Technical Analysis

... Is Mostly Bullshit

Why Flipping a Coin Is a Better Strategy than Using Technical Analysis in the Financial, Stock, and Forex Markets

By Tim Morris

Copyright © 2021
All Rights Reserved.
ISBN: 9781651868577
Published by ZML Corp LLC

Table of Contents

Disclaimer 3

Introduction 5

Chapter 1: Ways to Analyze the Market 9

Chapter 2: Textbook Technical Analysis 15

Chapter 3: Issues With Technical Analysis 35

Chapter 4: The Final Verdicts 59

Bonus Chapter: Japanese Candlesticks 73

Conclusion 77

Disclaimer

This book is for entertainment and informational purposes only. The creator of this book is not an investment advisory service, a registered investment advisor, or a broker-dealer and does not advise clients on which securities they should buy or sell for themselves. It must be understood that a very high degree of risk is involved in trading stocks. The publisher of this book, and the affiliates of the publisher assume no responsibility or liability for trading and investment results. It should not be assumed that the methods, techniques, or indicators presented in this book will be profitable nor that they will not result in losses. In addition, the indicators, strategies, rules and all other features of the information presented are provided for information and educational purposes only and should not be construed as investment advice. Investors and traders must always consult with their licensed financial advisors and tax advisors before partaking in any investment.

The author and publisher have no affiliation with any brokers or websites listed in this book. The author receives compensation for the affiliate links used in the book. Copyright © 2021, all rights reserved. Written by Tim Morris. Published by ZML Corp LLC.

Introduction

Hello, my name is Tim Morris! If you've read any of my other books, you know I provide you the unfiltered truth about the stock market, and don't blow sunshine into your rear. With that said, I felt it was about time I wrote a book going over technical analysis (TA). In this book, I'm not only going to show you what the "textbooks" say about the topic, but also going to provide real world analysis.

While certain aspects of technical analysis are beneficial, I'd say most of it is unfortunately bullshit, and the only people making money from it are the ones selling the courses, chatroom subscriptions, and books on the subject. Let me first go over my experience with technical analysis.

When you first get started learning about the stock market, there is a lot of information thrown at you at once. Being a beginner, you have no idea what is real and what is fake. When I first got started, I was told the two main ways traders analyze the markets are with fundamental and technical analysis.

At the time, fundamental analysis seemed too complicated for me. You had to dig through balance sheets, statements, earnings... who wants to do that? Technical analysis seemed so easy. You find patterns on a chart, buy when the stock hits a certain point, and make a ton of money. I was going to be a millionaire in no time! I bought a $400 course on technical analysis and started learning. I then signed up for a $200 a month subscription service from a trader who claimed to be a technical analysis expert.

After using my new found knowledge from the TA course I took, as well as following the "expert" trader for many months, I was down well over $5,000 in stocks, not including the subscription fees. What happened? I thought TA was supposed to make me a millionaire? I decided I was just not a great chartist and quit using TA.

Fast forward a few years, now having much more knowledge and experience under my belt in the stock market, and I came across an article on the internet. The article made the point that many of the patterns found in technical analysis are not unique to stocks, but also appear in charts from just about any subject you can think of. Charts like baby birth trends, suicide rates, car accidents and more were all showing the same patterns that were supposed to make me a millionaire. How could this be? Buyers and sellers are supposed to be controlling these charts, not babies! I started doing more research.

As I dug deeper and deeper into technical analysis, none of it made sense. What makes a chart pattern go in the direction it is intended to? Why would a pattern which appears on a chart have any correlation to the way a stock price moves? Do buyers and sellers make it happen? The universe's energy? Babies? As I continued doing my research, I kept finding loads of "experts" selling how-to courses on technical analysis. However, what I failed to find where people who had actually made their wealth from technical analysis. As I talk about in my free report *Crush the Market*, 95% of hedge fund managers fail to beat the general market. Shouldn't these traders, the smartest Ivy

League graduates in the country, shouldn't they be able to use technical analysis successfully? I found even the people who had invented technical analysis indicators weren't able to use their own indicators successfully.

It was at this moment that I finally had an epiphany. Did you know during the California gold rush in the 1800s, the people who ended up making the most money were the ones selling the mining equipment? And just like the gold rush, the people teaching TA courses, and even the people making TA indicators, weren't making money *using* technical analysis.

Everyone wants to be rich right now and it's easy to sell dreams. The internet provides a cloak of invisibility. No one really knows if you're an expert. It has been this way for years with real estate seminars, penny stock courses, and other get rich quick schemes. It finally all made sense to me… technical analysis was bullshit!

Chapter 1
Ways to Analyze the Market

Deciding on what direction you think an individual stock will go, or the market in general, traders have two methodologies to choose from:

1. Fundamental Analysis
2. Technical Analysis

Now obviously this is not an inclusive list of all methodologies in existence, but these two are the most common you will come across.

Fundamental Analysis

Fundamental analysis involves analyzing a business' finances to make a determination if said company is a good investment. It also takes into consideration company management, consumer sentiment, the economy, the competition, and a variety of other factors.

The ultimate goal of fundamental analysis is to identify stocks which are "undervalued," and buy them at a point in which they will increase in price and make a profit.

As you may be aware, fundamental analysis is quite broad, so there are a number of different techniques traders use which would be considered "fundamental analysis." The main takeaway here though is many traders in history have used fundamental analysis successfully to acquire great wealth. Names like Warren Buffett and Peter Lynch may ring a bell, but most hedge funds also use fundamental analysis as their primary methodology to invest. And of course, many lay traders you've never heard of use fundamental analysis. I'd also say fundamental analysis would be considered more of a science than an art. As in it is more quantitative (e.g. data, numbers) than qualitative (e.g. descriptive, can't be measured).

I'm not claiming you will get rich from fundamental analysis, nor am I saying it is easy or always works correctly, but I **am** saying it is a much better method of analyzing stocks than the next methodology I am about to go over. You can learn more about fundamental analysis from Investopedia here (linkpony.com/fa).

Technical Analysis

Technical analysis is a methodology which involves analyzing chart patterns in an effort to predict future price movements. What's unique about technical analysis is traders who analyze charts, known as "chartered market technicians" (CMTs), claim technical analysis can work for any market and in any time frame. This would include stocks, options, futures, commodities, and forex markets. All of which have different types of traders, hours, etc. But does technical analysis hold up to scrutiny? Can it really do everything these technicians claim it can? That's for you to decide after reading this book.

Something to note is a private company called the "CMT Association" offers a certificate for traders to become "chartered market technicians," for the small price of $1,500. When you pass your test, you receive a plaque to go on your wall, a gold star, and this private company gets $1,500 of your money. The CMT Association asserts companies like Wells Fargo and Charles Schwab are dying to hire CMTs. For some reason I don't believe this.

There are claims of traders who have successfully used technical analysis to make great sums of money, such as in Jack Schwager's book, *Market Wizards*. However, I don't find there's any names in history that stand out in traders' minds as "technical analysis kings." I'd also argue that trades made by such persons were most likely not pure technical analysis, but rather a combination of factors.

◆ ◆ ◆

Other Market Hypotheses

There are a number of other hypotheses related to the stock market; I will go over the most common ones here. These hypotheses throw shade on both fundamental and technical analysis, as they state neither can reliably predict the price movement of stocks. All of these hypotheses have their supporters and critics.

Efficient Market Hypothesis (EMH)

This hypothesis, originally created by Ph.D economist Eugene Fama, states that all known information is reflected in the price of a stock, meaning it's trading at a fair value at any given time. This would imply that it's impossible to consistently "beat the market," as markets can only react to new information. While I would argue some individuals have effectively beaten the market, there could be other reasons for their success. As in luck, timing, inside knowledge, etc. This hypothesis is quite interesting when you add the fact that so many hedge funds fail to beat the market.

Random Walk Hypothesis (RWH)

Similar to the EMH, the RWH states markets cannot be beaten, and are simply random movements over time. While I don't completely agree with this theory, it definitely has its truths. Stocks do seem rather random and trying to pick their short term price direction can be difficult. This hypothesis makes technical analysis much more doubtful, especially once we get into the coin flip experiment, which we will go over later in the book.

Noisy Market Hypothesis (NMH)

I think this is my favorite of the hypotheses. The NMH goes against the EMH, and states that noise, in the form of speculators, momentum traders, insiders, and institutions, can influence a stock's price and create "noise" in the markets. Thus the market is not always efficient. This theory also takes into account groupthink, the bandwagon effect, and the Abilene paradox.

As I'm sure you're aware, "noise" seems to definitely occur in the markets, and it is important to consider when trading. I mean look at Bitcoin. People were taking out loans against their homes to finance Bitcoin purchases when it reached $20,000 due to fear of missing out (FOMO) and the bandwagon effect. This certainly would not be an "efficient market," meaning noise played a factor.

As a **token of appreciation** to my readers, I am providing my special report titled *Crush the Market* **absolutely free!** This report goes over 14 beneficial tips that will help you profit in the stock market. Just copy & paste the link below into your browser and it will be immediately emailed to you!

linkpony.com/crush

Chapter 2
Textbook Technical Analysis

This chapter is for those unfamiliar with the many patterns and indicators that make up technical analysis. I will go over each of them, explaining what classic TA theory teaches. Then in chapter 4, I will reveal my thoughts on each of these topics.

Here is a list of the topics we will be reviewing:

Patterns
1. Support/Resistance Lines
2. Head and Shoulders
3. Bull Pennants (Flags)
4. Rising/Falling Wedges
5. Cup and Handle
6. Double Top/Bottom
7. Triangles
8. Trendlines

Indicators
1. Fibonacci Retracement/Projection
2. Elliott Wave Theory
3. Moving Averages
4. RSI
5. MACD
6. Bollinger Bands
7. Stochastics
8. Divergence
9. Volume

Patterns

The first topic we will be going over is patterns. Patterns fall into three categories: reversal, continuation, and neutral patterns. TA theory states that when these patterns appear on a chart, they will likely move in their intended direction, and thus you can make money trading them. The images on the next few pages will provide you a better idea of the theory behind each pattern. Each pattern is listed in its respected category, while also showing the correct entry point, target price, and stop-loss location.

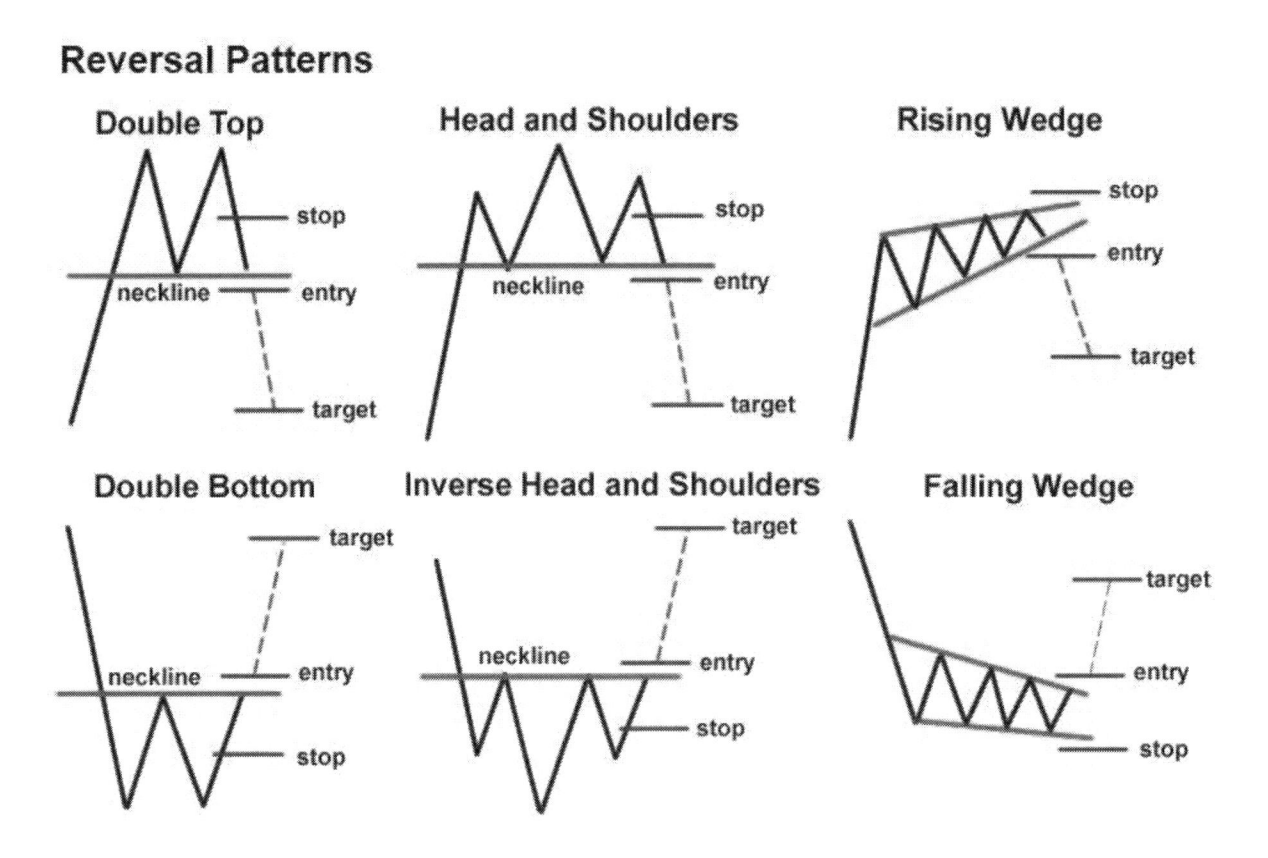

Reversal Patterns

Double Top

Head and Shoulders

Rising Wedge

Double Bottom

Inverse Head and Shoulders

Falling Wedge

Continuation Patterns

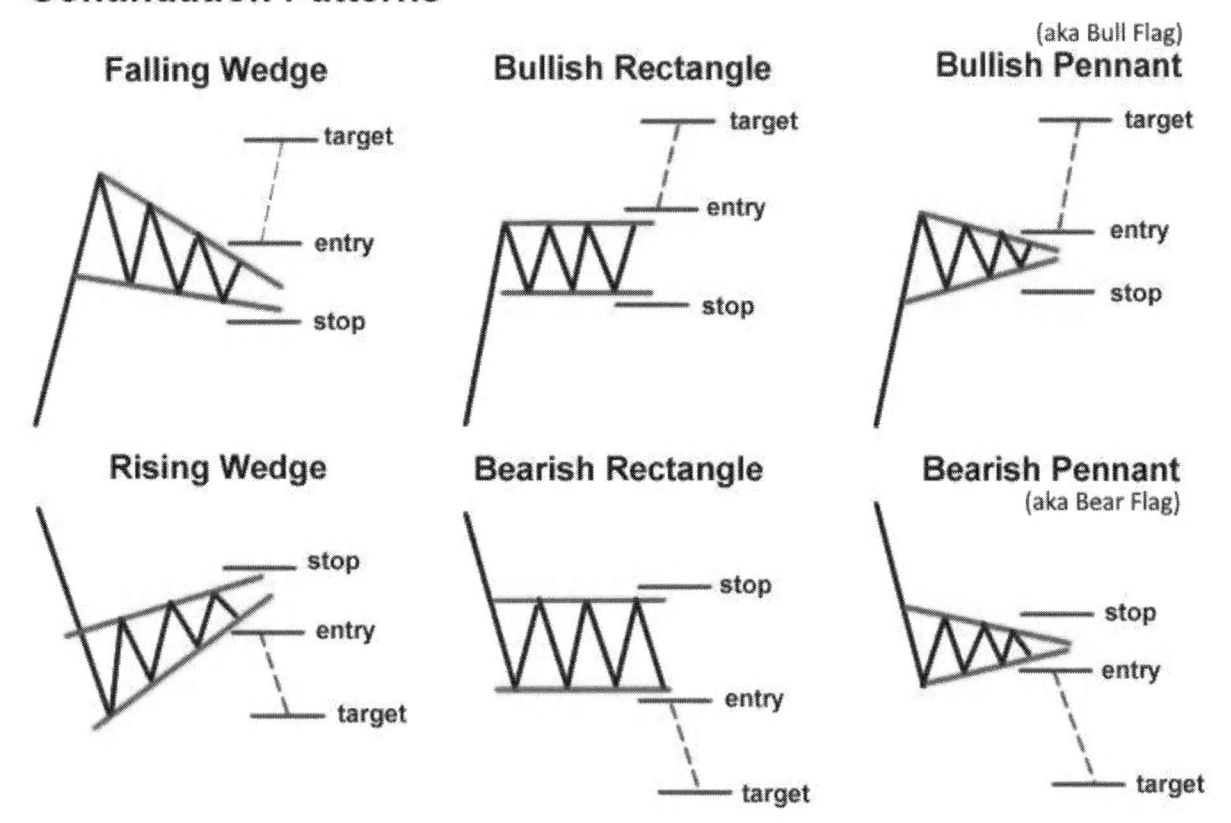

Falling Wedge
- target
- entry
- stop

Bullish Rectangle
- target
- entry
- stop

Bullish Pennant
(aka Bull Flag)
- target
- entry
- stop

Rising Wedge
- stop
- entry
- target

Bearish Rectangle
- stop
- entry
- target

Bearish Pennant
(aka Bear Flag)
- stop
- entry
- target

Continuation Patterns

Ascending Triangle

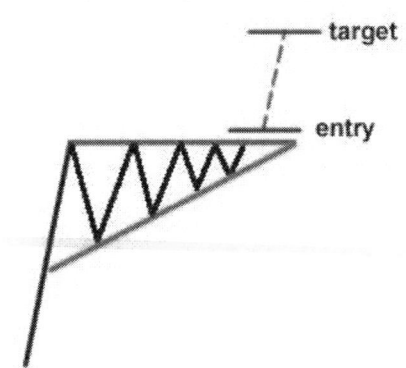

Descending Triangle

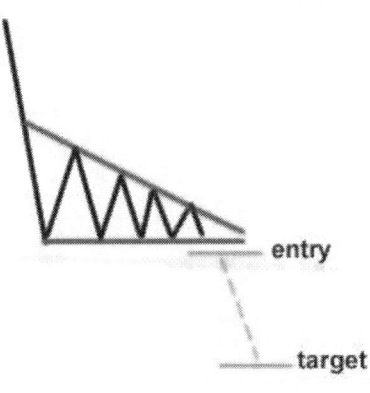

Cup and Handle

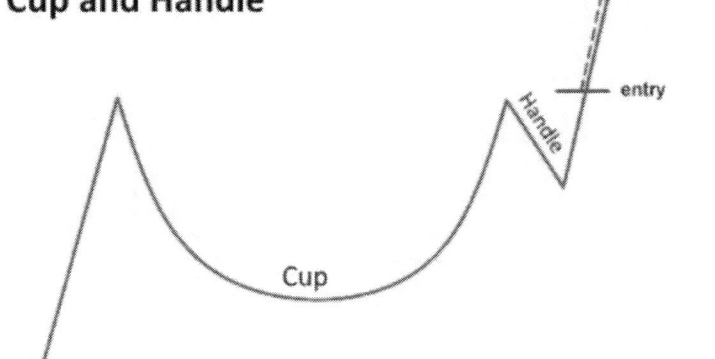

Neutral Pattern

Symmetrical Triangle

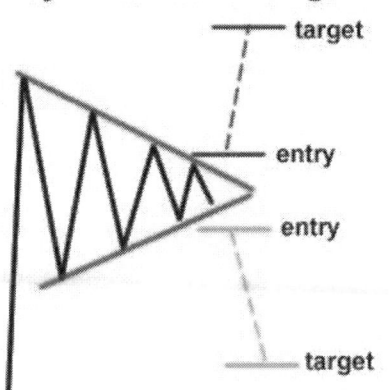

Resistance & Support

◆ ◆ ◆

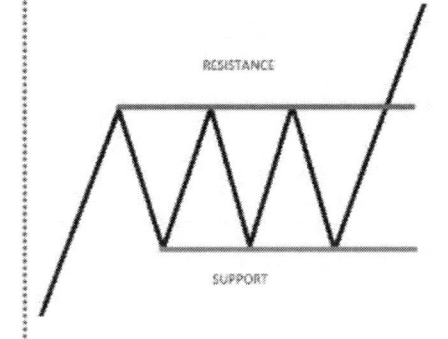

Indicators

Fibonacci Retracement

Fibonacci was an Italian mathematician who was working on controlling a population of rabbits. He ended up coming up what is now known as the "Fibonacci Sequence." The sequence goes as follows:

1, 1, 2, 3, 5, 8, 13, 21, 34, 55, 89, 144

Each number is the sequence is the previous two numbers added together. When you divide each number by the previous number, you then get this sequence:

- *1 / 1 = 1*
- *2 / 1 = 2*
- *3 / 2 = 1.5*
- *and so on up to 144 / 89 = 1.6179*

As you can see, each division equation higher in the sequence gets closer and closer to 1.618, which is known as the "golden ratio." This pattern of numbers Fibonacci discovered is a pattern that occurs frequently throughout nature. This is shown in the image on the next page.

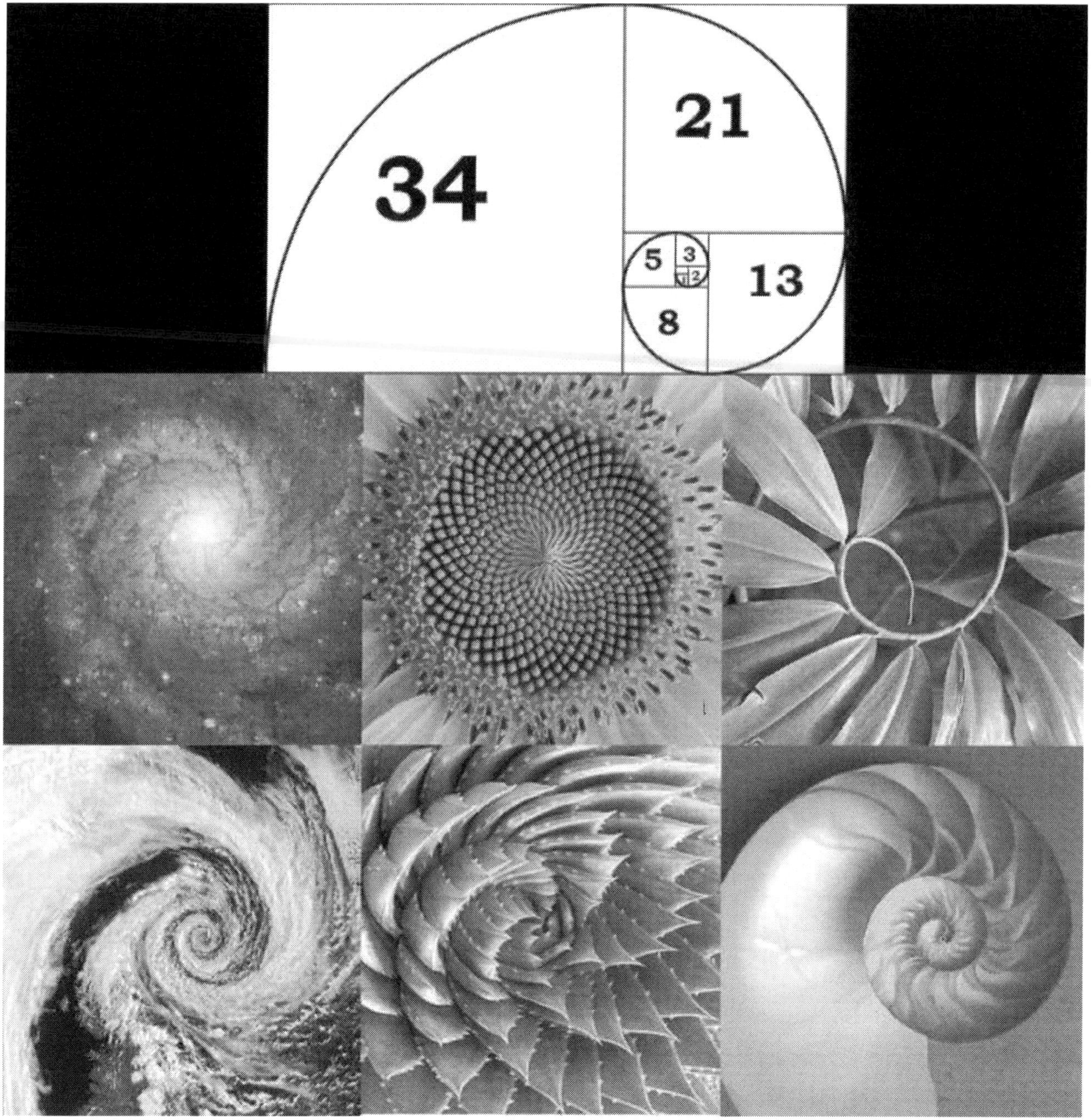
34
21
13
8
5
3
2

Someone, making the connection between the stock market and nature, decided the Fibonacci ratio could be applied to the stock market. The most prominent ways technicians currently implement this are with two tools: Fibonacci retracement and Fibonacci projection (with many more spin-offs that have since been made). We'll start with Fibonacci retracement. This is the theory that after a large gain (or loss), a stock will pull back to a common Fibonacci point (31.2% or 61.8%), before heading higher or lower. As in these points serve as places the stock will "pivot," which can be utilized as buy or sell points to make money. The points correlate with the "golden ratio" number, as 31.2% is 0.618 below 1, and 61.8% is 0.618 above 0. Let me show you an example on the daily chart of AMD.

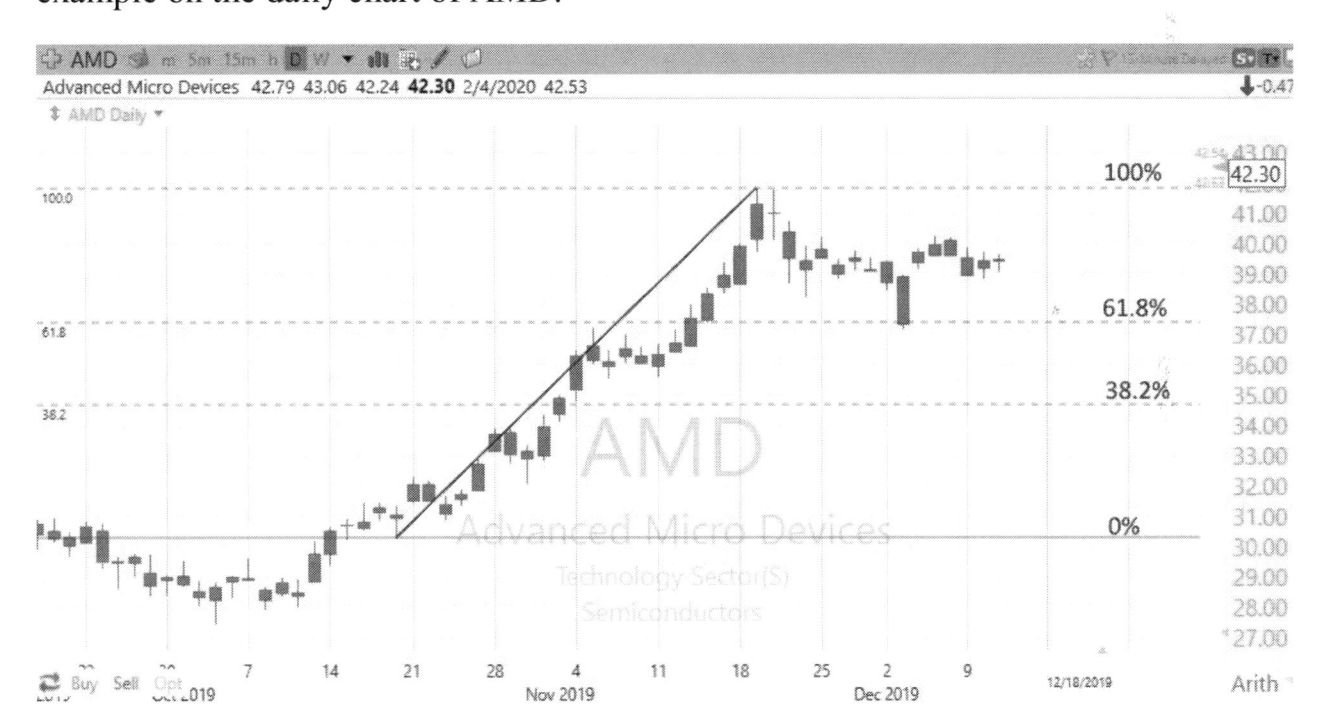

As you can see there is a line which connects the 0% point (low), and the 100% point

21

(high). Between these two points, the dotted "Fibonacci" lines are then calculated. Once the stock starts moving downward from its high, it bounces off the dotted 61.8% Fibonacci line, and then moves higher. The theory states these Fibonacci lines can be used in any market and any time frame, as well as in upward and downward trends.

Fibonacci projection is just a variation of this theory, and purports to predict future pivot points using the power of Fibonacci. Here again you choose a low and high point, and then use the future Fibonacci ratios above 100% (161.8%, 261.8%, 423.6%, etc.) as your pivot points. These are calculated by adding the previous two numbers in the sequence together. As in 61.8% + 100% = 161.8%, 161.8% + 100% = 261.8%, etc. Here is an example on the weekly chart of the leveraged ETF TQQQ.

I chose a low and high point, and then as you can see, the dotted Fibonacci lines at and above 100% appear to serve as resistance/support locations that the stock pivots around.

Elliott Wave Theory (EWT)

Ralph Elliott, stricken with an illness and forced to retire, wanted to find something to occupy his time. It was the 1930's and, having an interest in the stock market, Mr. Elliott started researching decades worth of stock charts. Looking through many different stock charts in many different time frames, Ralph proclaimed he noticed a consistent pattern which occurred. He coined this pattern the "Elliott Wave Theory." This theory started to pick up steam when Ralph was able to call a market bottom in 1935, and continues to be used by chartists to this day.

The theory states stocks, in all time frames, move in 5-3 waves. Five of the waves move with the trend, called the "motive phase," and three of the waves move against the trend called the "corrective phase." Let me show you an example in a chart of what the EWT is supposed to look like.

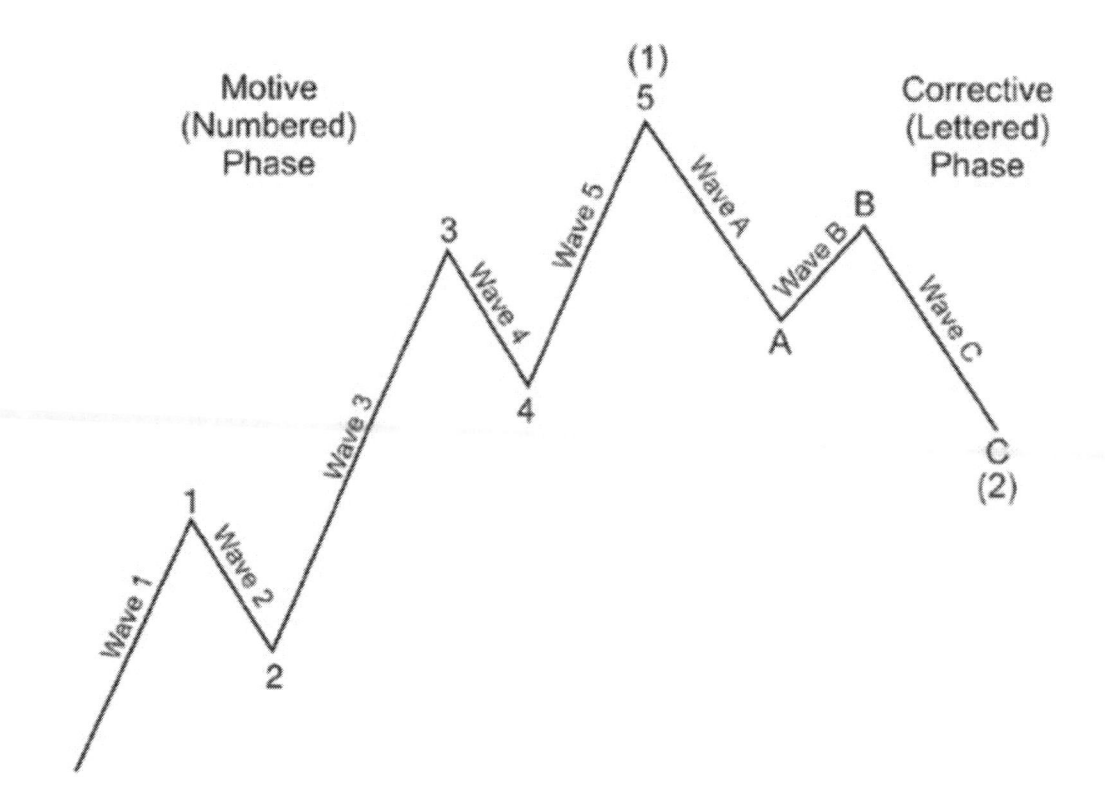

This chart shows a stock in an uptrend, but it could be flipped upside down as well, to be used in a downtrending stock. Ralph Elliott stated if a trader could find the correct 5-3 wave count in a chart, he could accurately predict the future movement of said stock.

Moving Averages (MA)

A moving average is displayed in the form of a line on a chart. It takes the last "X" number of periods (hours, days, weeks), depending on what number you indicate, and then averages them together to form a line displayed on a chart. For example if someone placed a 50 MA line on an hourly chart, it would show the last 50 hours of the stock price in the form of a line. If someone placed this same 50 MA on a daily chart, it would show the last 50 days of stock price in the form of a line.

The most common periods used are the 50, 100, and 200 moving averages. There are also multiple *types* of MAs traders can use, with the most common being the simple and exponential MAs. A simple moving average (SMA) weights all periods before hand equally on a chart. An exponential moving average (EMA) places more weight on the most recent periods. Let me show you an example of both the 50 SMA and EMA on the daily chart of SPY.

Many technicians will use a moving average line as a support/resistance level when deciding on when to trade stocks. MA crossovers are also commonly used by

25

technicians as an indication of a trend change. Two MA crossover examples would be the death cross and the golden cross. The death cross is when the 50 MA line crosses below the 200 MA line. The golden cross is when the 50 MA line crosses above the 200 MA line.

Relative Strength Index (RSI)

Introduced in the late 1970's by J. Welles Wilder Jr., RSI is a momentum indicator that claims to be able to detect overbought and oversold conditions of a stock. On a chart, it is shown as a number between 0 and 100. Most charting software defaults to > 70 being overbought, and < 30 being oversold, with "14" being the look back period. This look back period is the number used when equating the RSI. For example, on a daily chart RSI is calculated with the last 14 days, on an hourly chart the last 14 hours, on a 1 minute chart the last 14 minutes, etc.

While you don't need to know the actual equation, as you'll never need to calculate it on your own, just understand RSI is basically averaging the gains and losses of the last 14 periods, which is then shown in the RSI chart. Many technicians also place a 5 day SMA on the RSI chart, as a crossover is said to indicate a trend reversal. I have an example on the next page with a daily chart of the stock Coca Cola (KO).

27

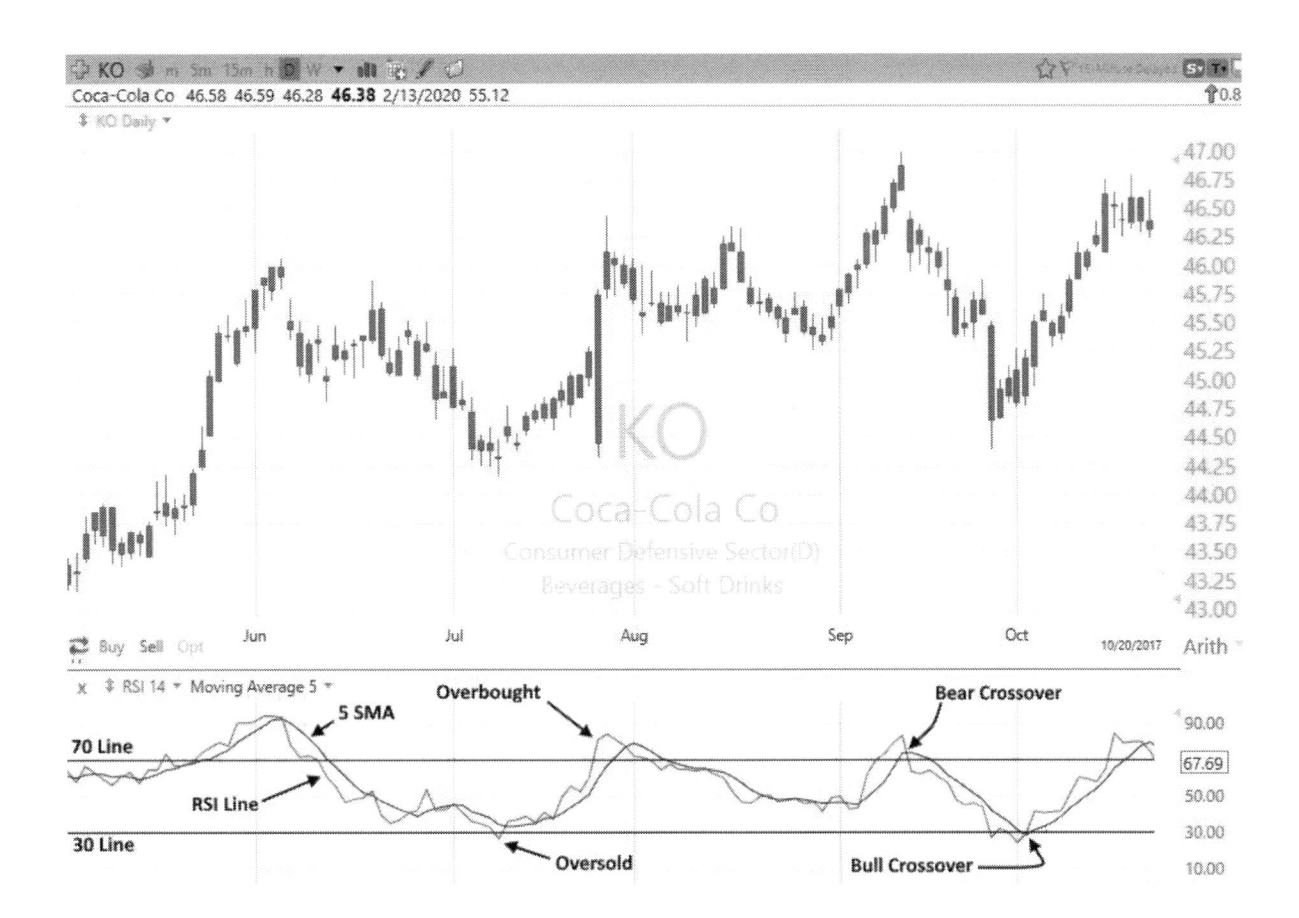

Moving Average Convergence Divergence (MACD)

Created in the 1970s by Gerald Appel, the MACD is a momentum indicator which claims to show when a stock will reverse in trend. It is calculated by subtracting the 26 period EMA from the 12 period EMA, which is shown as a line on a chart. Many traders also add a 9 EMA to the MACD chart, which is known as the "signal line." This signal line is then used as a buy/sell signal. As in, when the MACD crosses above the signal line, it is a buy signal. And when the MACD crosses below the signal line, it is a sell signal. Here is an example with a 15 minute chart of the stock Starbucks (SBUX).

Bollinger Bands

Invented in the early 1980's by John Bollinger, two bands are plotted on a chart which are 2 standard deviations away from the 20 period SMA. Stocks are said to trade inside the Bollinger Bands 90% of the time. Contracting Bollinger Bands are said to usually be followed by large volatility, though the direction is not known. If a stock moves above the upper Bollinger Band, it is said to be overbought. If a stock moves below the lower Bollinger Band, it is said to be oversold. Let me show you an example on the daily chart of Sirius XM (SIRI).

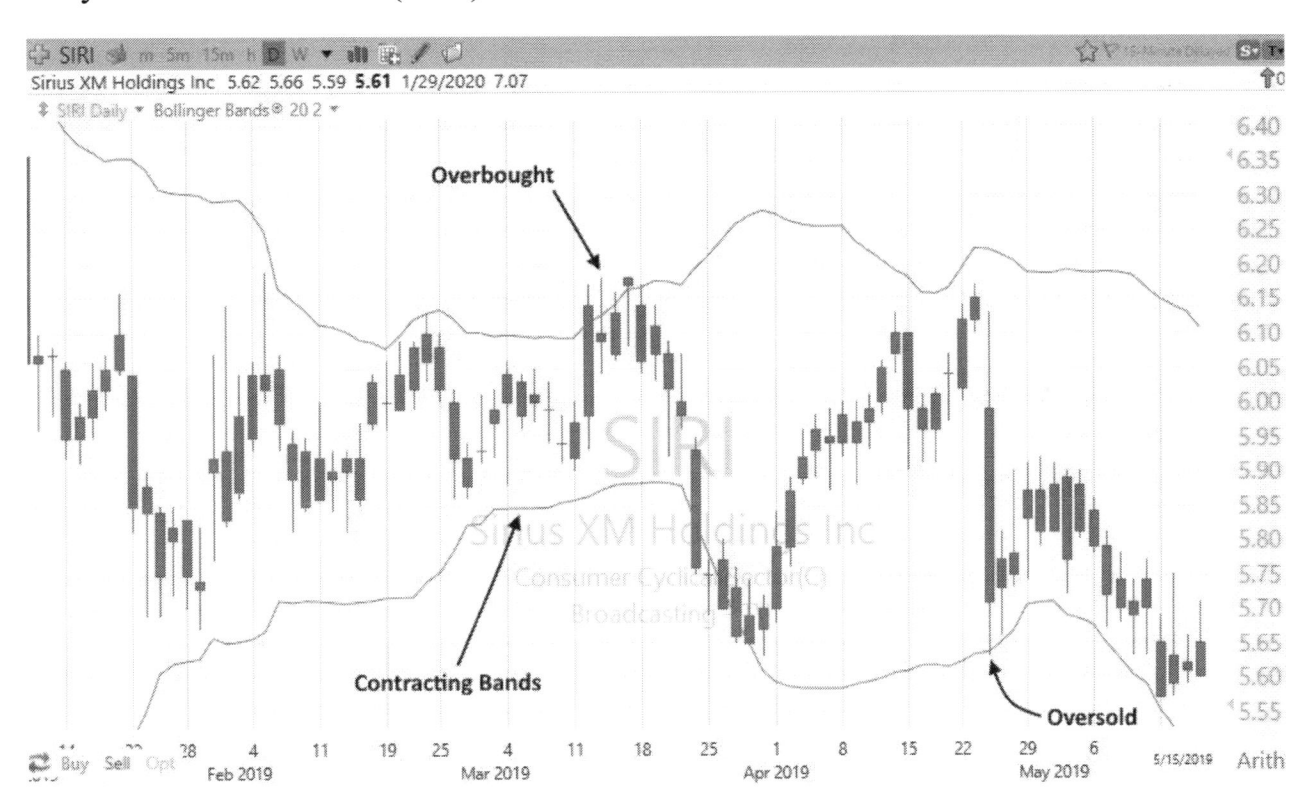

Stochastics

Developed in the 1950s, the "Stochastics Oscillator" is an indicator which claims to show overbought and oversold conditions. Similar to RSI, it ranges from 0 – 100, with a 14 day lookback period. With Stochastics, 20 and 80 are commonly used as the oversold and overbought levels. Many technicians also put a 3 day SMA on their Stochastics chart, as an intersection between the two lines is thought to predict a trend reversal. Let me show you an example on a weekly chart of PayPal (PYPL).

Divergence

Divergence can occur on a variety of indicators, with RSI being just one example. The claim is that if a trend in the stock contradicts a trend in the indicator, a reversal in the trend of the stock is eminent. Let's look at an example showing divergence with RSI, on a daily chart of Roku (ROKU).

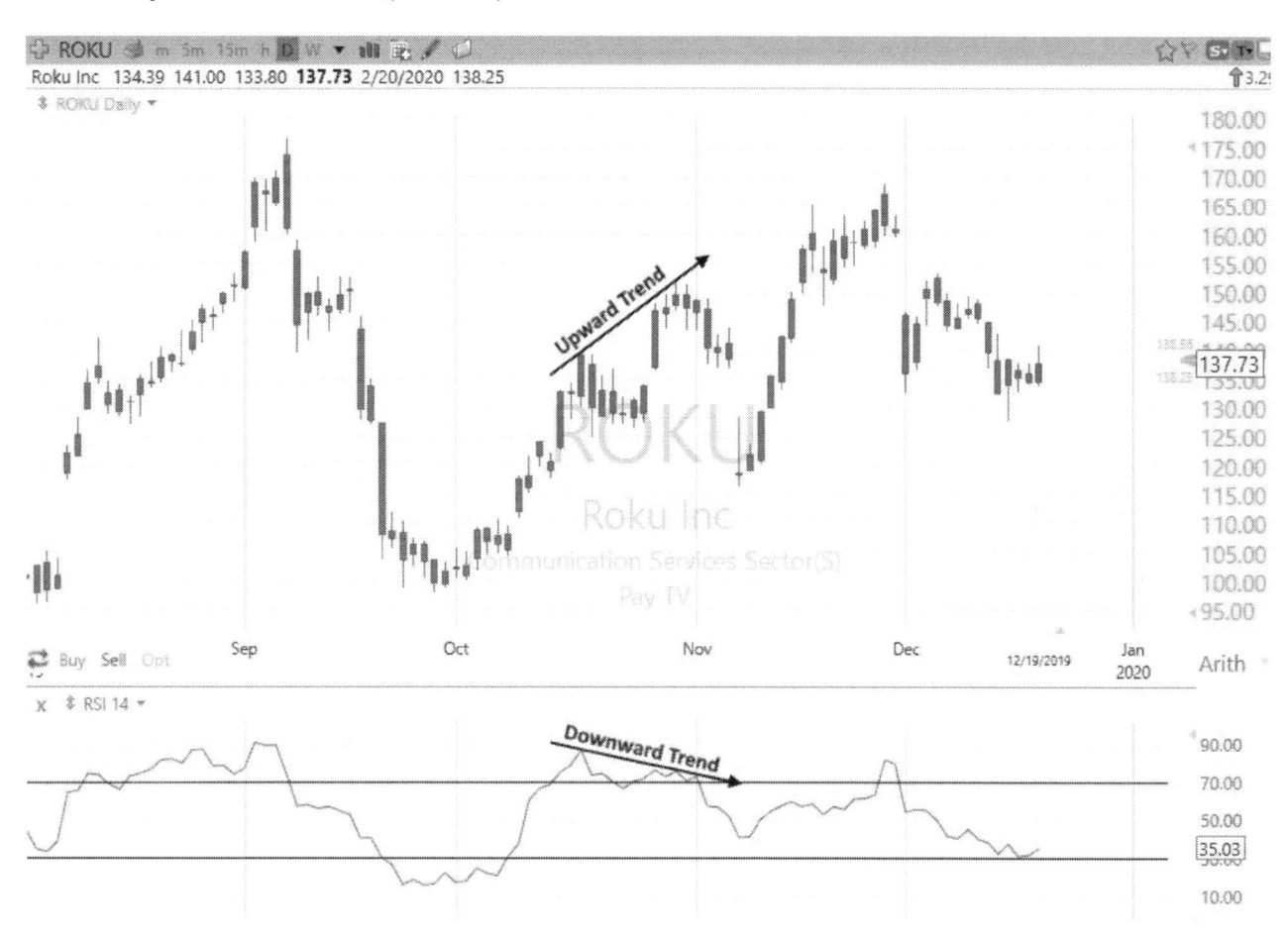

31

Volume

Volume is just the number of trades that have taken place in a given time frame. For example, when looking at a daily chart, each volume bar at the bottom of the chart is one day's worth of volume. When looking at a 5 minute chart, each volume bar at the bottom is 5 minutes worth of volume, and so on. The rationale behind using volume as an indicator is if an influx of traders are coming into the market at a particular point, the prevailing trend will most likely continue. Let me show you an example of how volume is displayed with an hourly chart of General Electric (GE).

As you can see, the volume is displayed in the bottom of the chart in the form of bars. Each bar in this chart corresponds with the number of trades which occurred in each hour period. You'll see there is a 1 and 2 labeled on the chart. The bar next to "1" had over 20 million trades within an hour. The bar next to "2" had about 15 million trades within an hour. You'll also see that at bar 1, a large influx of sellers came in, which resulted in the stock moving downward for many periods afterwards.

Chapter 3
Issues With Technical Analysis

So are these patterns and indicators real? Does TA truly work as claimed? The short answer is no. There are unfortunately a number of flaws in the TA theory, many of which you may have never heard of. This chapter will give you a better idea as to why my opinion of TA is so negative, and the reasons it is a fictitious practice. And it's not just me; many in academia also consider technical analysis to be pseudoscience, with no real basis in fact. Famed economist Burton Malkiel has made the comparison of technical analysis to "astrology." What's your sign?

Data Snooping

Data snooping, also known as data dredging and hindsight bias, relates to finding patterns in past data to prove a theory. This is a common technique in TA. For example, let's bring up a daily chart of the stock Snapchat (SNAP).

Here you'll notice I have 4 items labeled which would be considered TA patterns which appear to have positive outcomes.

1. Bullish Rectangle
2. Double Bottom
3. Double Top
4. Upward Trendlines

The issue is this is all past data, as in it's all in hindsight. How were you supposed to know that each of these would actually happen? It's one thing to look at past data on a chart, but it's another thing to actually be making trades in real time. If you've ever actually tried implementing technical analysis, you're very aware of this.

Now I want to show you the same chart, except this time with TA patterns that did not have beneficial results.

1. Failed Downward Trend
2. Failed Double Top
3. Failed Double Bottom
4. Failed Upward Trend
5. Failed Double Bottom
6. Failed Bullish Rectangle

As you can see it's easy to look for data that "proves" technical analysis, but had you actually been using TA throughout this time period without future data to reference, you very easily could have gotten into one of these failed TA patterns. Chartists will say things like "oh those are failed patterns" or "it doesn't work 100% of the time." I got news for you, a stock can only move up or down. So of course a pattern will sometimes

37

work, but this is likely the result of random movement (which the coin flip experiment will show later in the book). I would think using a strategy that "sometimes" works wouldn't be something I would want to be invested in.

Confirmation Bias

Confirmation bias is essentially looking for and making patterns in data where patterns don't actually occur, as well as dismissing data that doesn't confirm your own biases. The Wikipedia definition of confirmation bias is:

> *Confirmation bias is the tendency to search for, interpret, favor, and recall information in a way that confirms one's preexisting beliefs or hypotheses.*

For example, if you are a gun control advocate, you may look for charts and figures which prove an increase in guns results in an increase in shootings. But you may dismiss data showing towns that have a large number of guns, with a low number of shootings. As in you are just looking for data that confirms your beliefs.

This plays a big role in technical analysis, and goes hand in hand with data snooping. You understand what different TA patterns look like, and then you start actively noticing and looking for them in charts. For example, you know what a double top is, and then actively start seeing it in charts. What you don't see is the many failed potential double tops that could have happened but didn't. Many times chartists will go to extreme measures to draw out patterns that really shouldn't be considered, but due to confirmation bias they interpret them as relevant. Here's an example. First I will show you a chart with what a classic head and shoulders pattern is supposed to look like.

Head and Shoulders

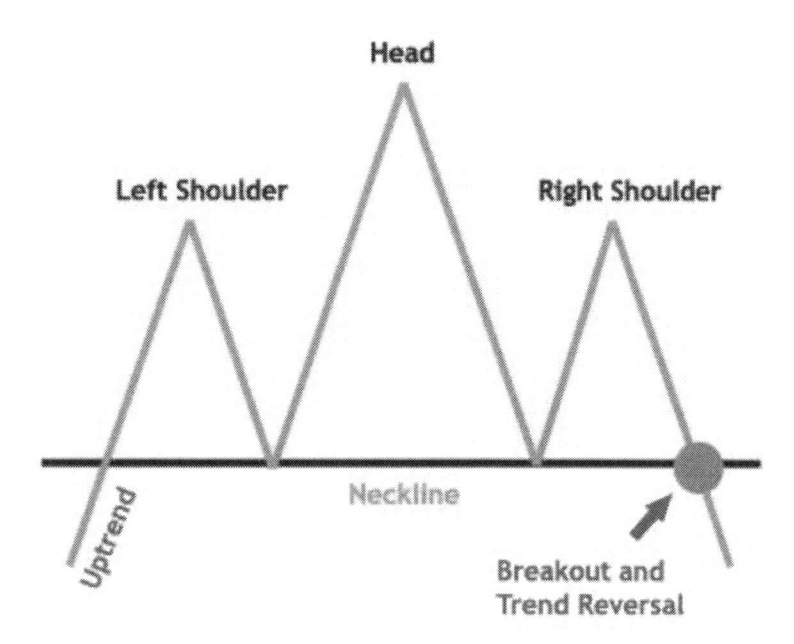

As you can see, there is a clear left shoulder, head, and right shoulder. This pattern is supposed to indicate said stock will soon fall below the original breakout point and reverse its trend. Now let me show you a montage of charts collected from the internet, drawn by those practicing TA, which are also supposed to be "head and shoulders" patterns.

As you can see, rules go out the window and anything that remotely resembles shoulders and a head becomes an H&S pattern. It doesn't matter if the neckline is flat, up, or down, if the shoulders are misaligned, if the trendline goes through wicks, they begin making this pattern fit in any way they can. Then if said stock ends up fulfilling the destiny of the H&S pattern, they can say, "See, TA does work." However, if the stock goes in the wrong direction, they will say they misread the chart or it was a failed H&S. It becomes a win-win situation in that there is no "wrong" calculation with TA.

You may notice that in the montage on the previous page, there are a variety of different charts used. This presents another problem.

Subjective Nature of TA

Many technicians will argue TA is an art, not a science. As in charts are subjective, and it takes a true artist to be able to decipher the correct patterns being displayed. There is a big issue with this. Unlike fundamental analysis techniques, such as finding the P/E ratio of a company which is a tangible number, a chart is completely subjective to interpretation. Meaning while one person may see a head and shoulders pattern forming in a chart, another may see a cup and handle. One person may see a downward trend, another a falling wedge. It's all open to interpretation of what you see in the chart. But now let's add in different chart types.

As you know, there are a variety of charts you can inspect, with the most common being bar charts, candlestick charts, and line charts. Let's go over an example of this with the stock Advanced Micro Devices (AMD).

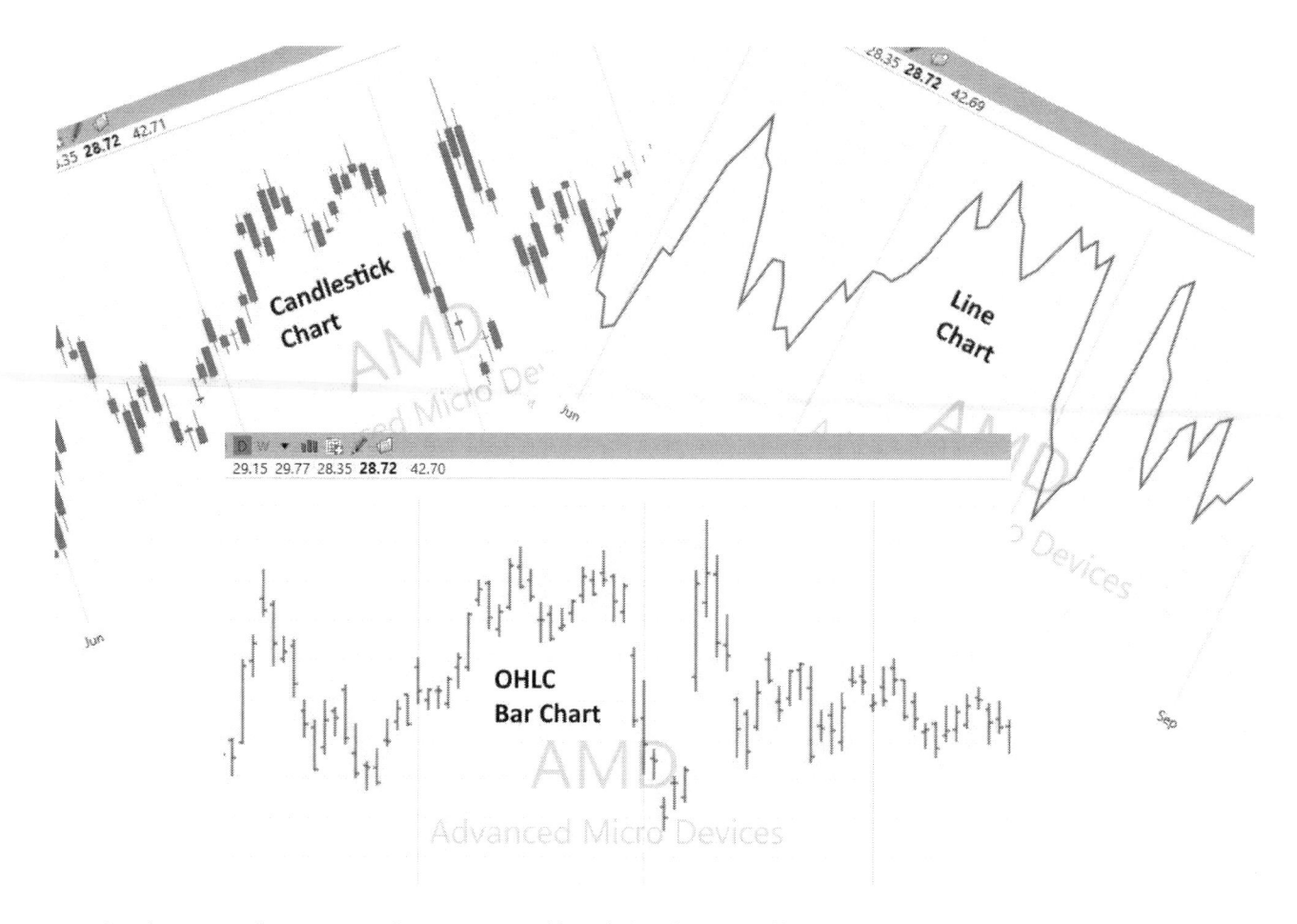

In the image above, we have a candlestick chart, a line chart, and an OHLC bar chart (open, high, low, close). All three are commonly used by chartists when referencing TA. However an issue presents itself, as all these charts are slightly different, meaning different patterns may form in each of them.

You may notice in the candlestick chart there are both wicks, as well as bodies in the candles displayed; these are not present in the line chart. This presents an issue in that different patterns can appear in each chart. Let me go over an example with the stock

Johnson and Johnson (JNJ).

43

Using the wicks from the candlesticks, we would be presented with only a double top formation. Using the line chart, we would be presented with only a double bottom formation. So which chart is correct? Which one should technicians use?

Another issue is contained within the candlestick charts. As you may be aware, the wicks are the high and low of the day, while the bodies are the open and close of the day. Many technicians use both wicks and candle bodies when drawing on charts, depending on what narrative fits with the pattern they are looking for. This lends to confirmation bias, in that they now have many more points on a chart to match their narrative. Let me show an example with the stock Fitbit (FIT).

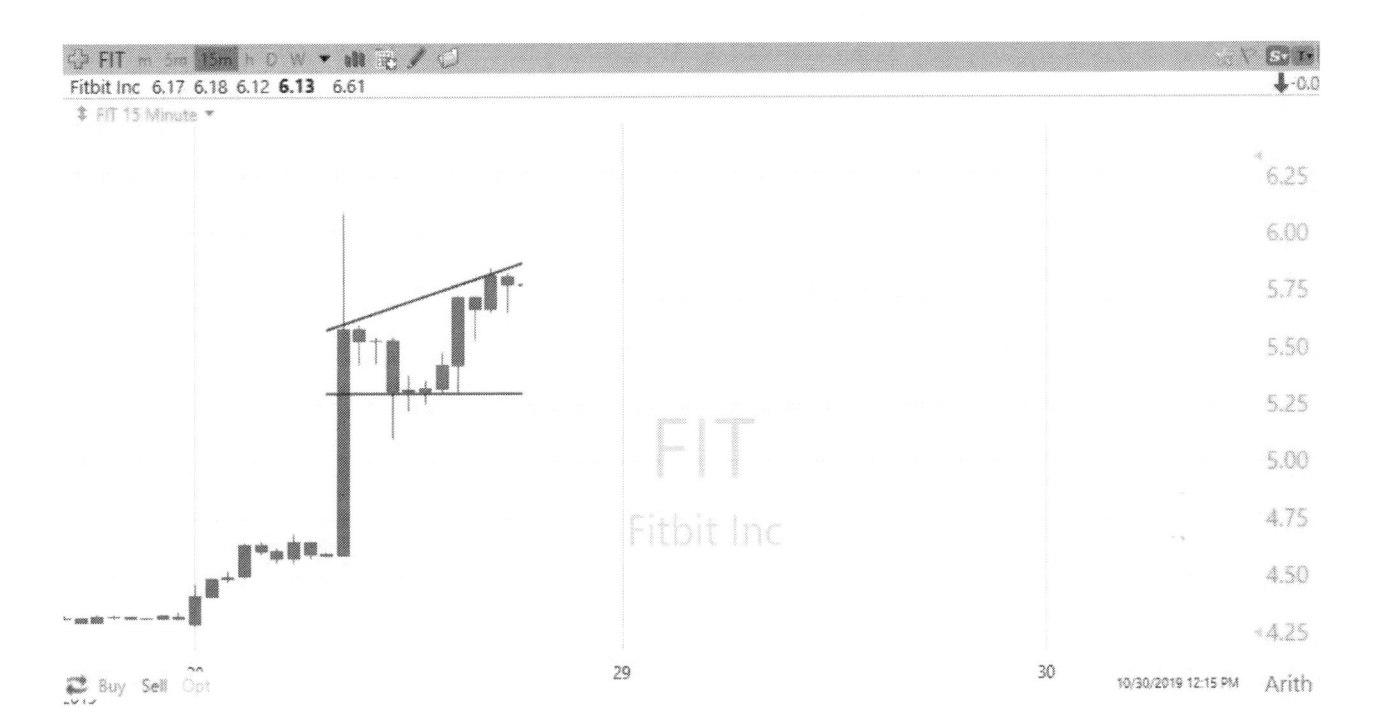

In the first chart, I drew lines using the candle wicks. The chart seems to be forming a symmetrical triangle pattern. In the second chart, I disregarded the wicks and only used the high and low bodies of the candles. Now we have a completely different formation, known as a "microphone," which has different entry/exit points. Again, which one is correct?

Different Time Frames and Markets

Chartists make the claim that TA works in a variety of markets and time frames. As in it can work in stocks, futures, commodities, and forex markets, as well as on 1 minute, 8 minute, 4 hour, 1 day, and 2 week charts. How is it possible for something to work

45

in so many different conditions?

A big issue with this premise is different time frames present completely different charts. As in, if you are looking at a 1 minute chart of a stock and compare it to a 5 minute chart, different, even contradicting TA patterns will start to present themselves. Which one should you use? Let me show you an example with two charts of UBER. The first will be a 5 minute chart, the second a 1 hour chart.

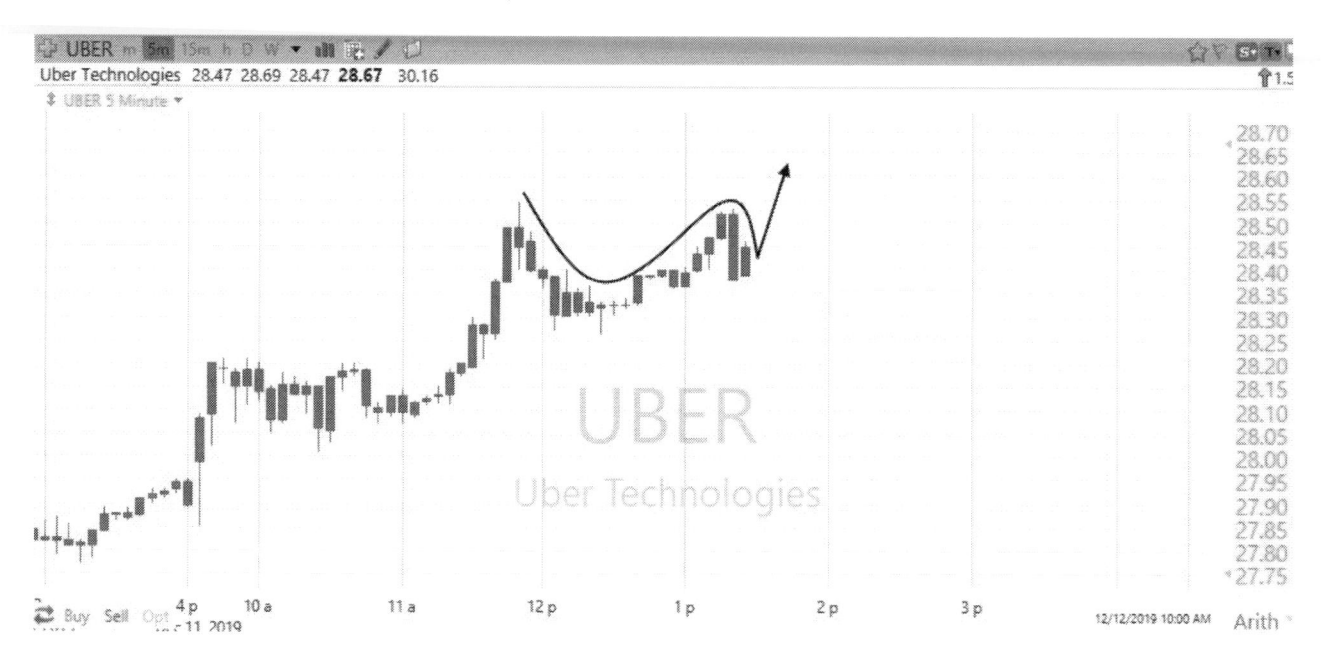

In this first 5 minute chart, we have a cup and handle pattern forming. This is where the stock makes a "U" cup formation, then moves down and up to form a handle. In this scenario, you would expect the stock to continue in an upward trend to complete the handle of the cup.

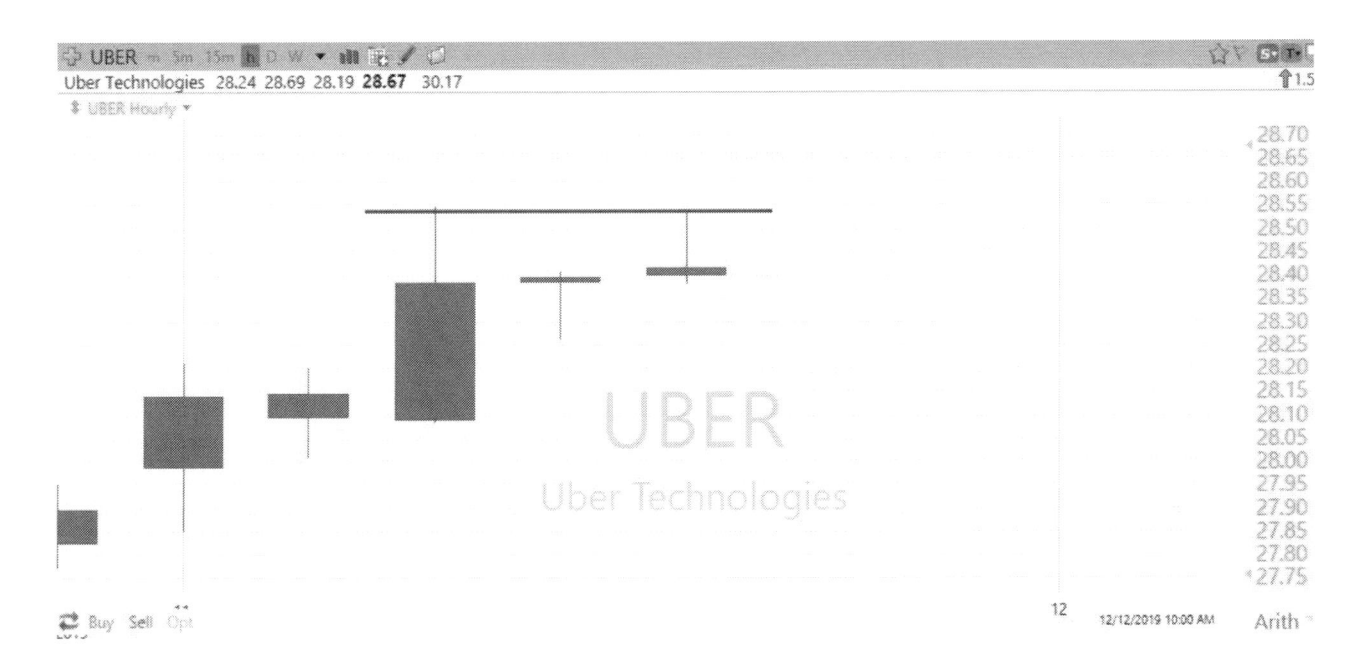

This is the same stock, on the exact same day, except now in an hourly chart. Here there is no cup and handle. Instead, we have what appears to be a double top forming. This means you would be betting the stock will soon go down in value.

So we have two charts, both showing the same stock on the same day, just in different time frames. And yet, these two charts show different patterns and have contradicting results. Which one should you choose? Is one better than the other?

Then we move to TA supposedly working in different markets. As in the patterns which form on a chart are not just limited to stocks, but can be applied in the forex, commodities, and futures markets. How? Why? What makes these patterns work? What moves a random pattern appearing on a chart in the proper direction? Is the universe's energy making these patterns go in their corresponding direction? As famed economist Burton Malkiel said, much of TA is essentially astrology in the markets.

Technical Patterns Appearing Everywhere

Many traders may not realize this, as it's not widely propagated, however TA patterns are not unique to the financial markets. These patterns appear in a number of charts that are completely unrelated to finance or buyers and sellers.

I am first going to show you a chart with no labels, but only the corresponding TA patterns that appear in the chart. I will then reveal the statistical data that correlates with said chart.

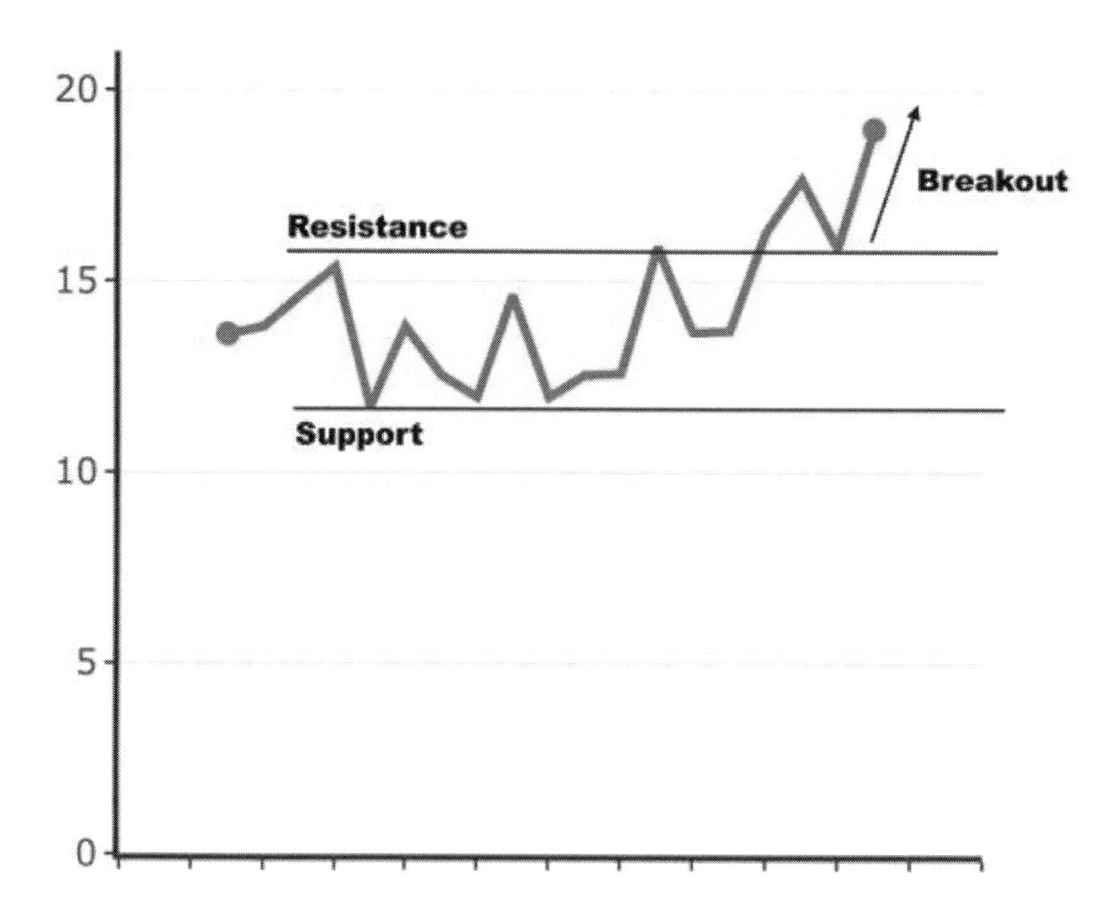

Here we have a chart showing clear support and resistance lines. Then when the pattern "breaks out," the resistance becomes support, which is a typical philosophy held by chartists. Now let's reveal what this is a chart of.

Suicide rate in Illinois
Number of suicides per 100,000 persons

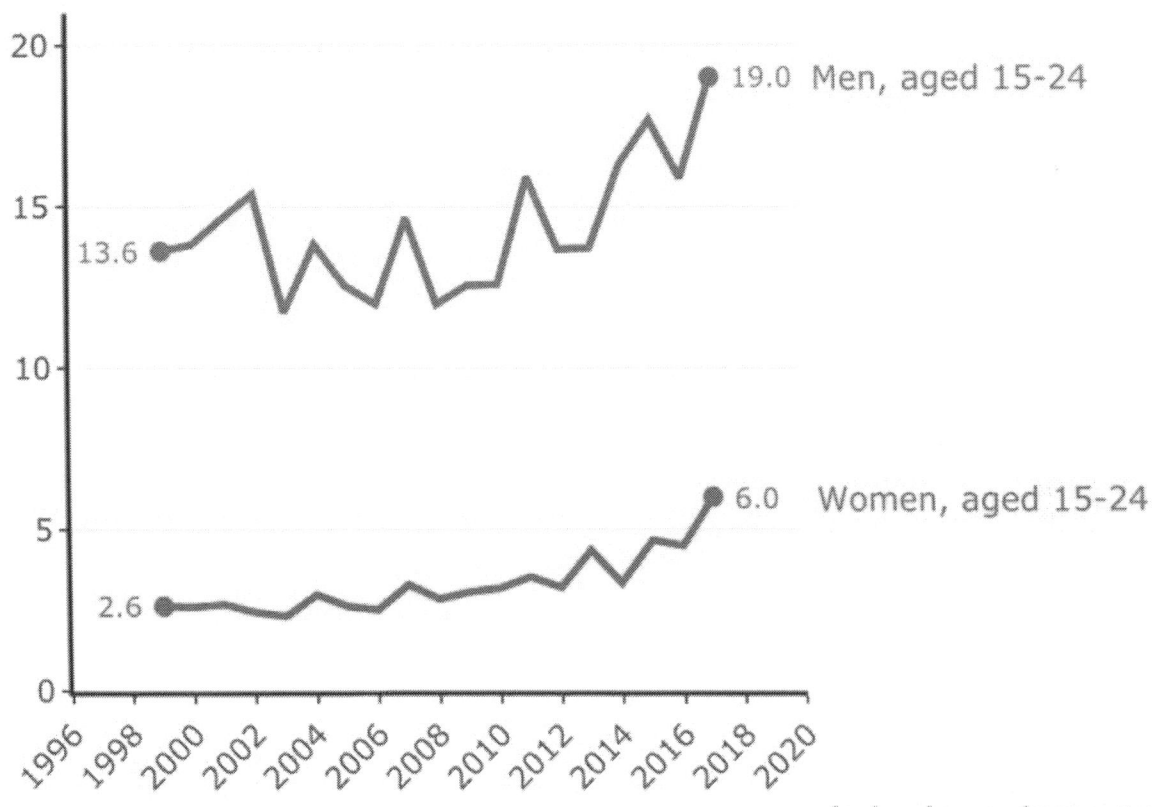

- 19.0 Men, aged 15-24
- 13.6
- 6.0 Women, aged 15-24
- 2.6

made by inspurious.com

This is actually a chart of suicide rates in the state of Illinois in the United States. So suicides also have support and resistance. Let's look at another chart.

49

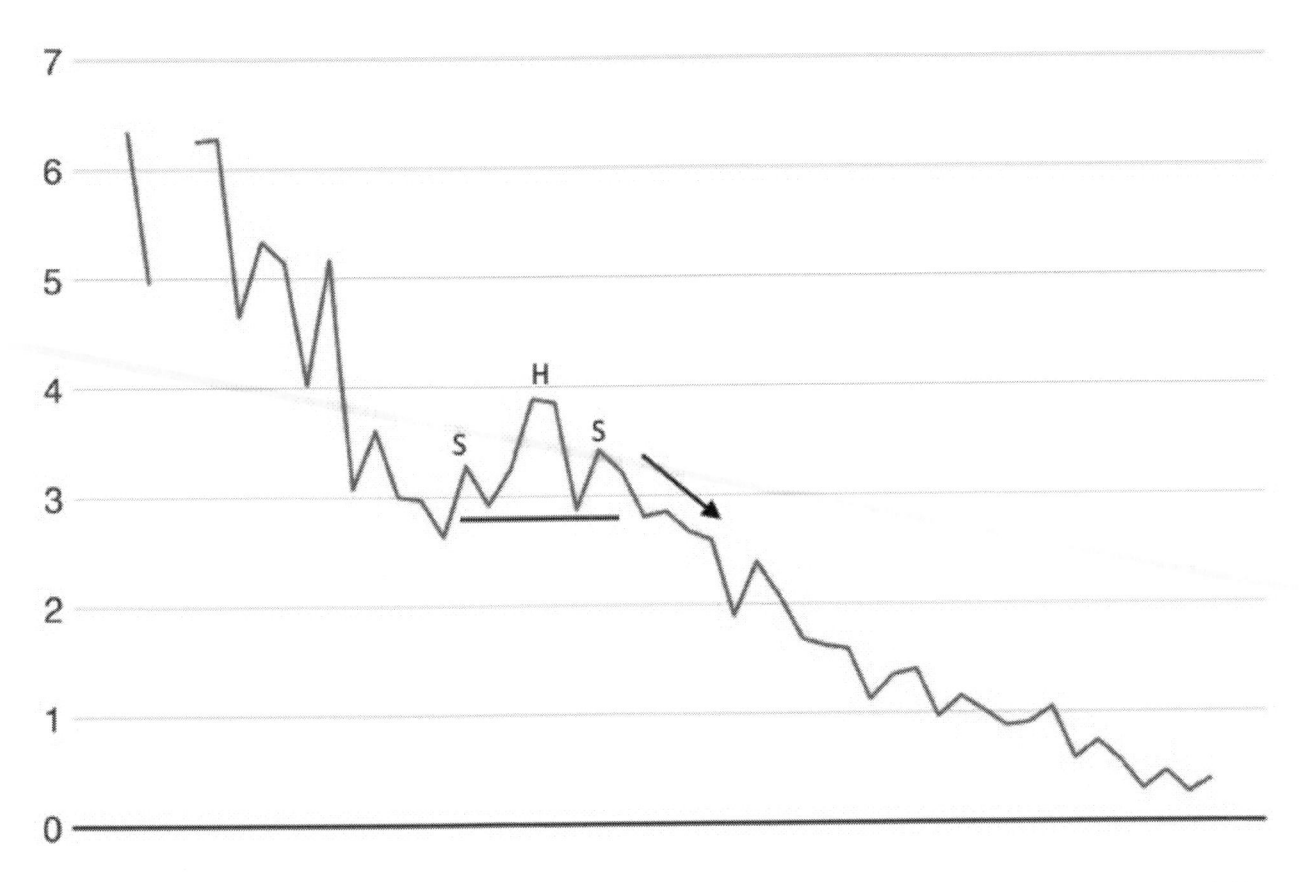

Here we have a clear head and shoulders pattern formation. We can see the neckline, the head, both shoulders, and then a breakdown lower once the pattern broke the neckline. This is a classic H&S pattern, and if you were to give this chart to a technician, they would say short that stock! Let's see what stock it is.

Flying has become much safer
Fatal accidents per million departures

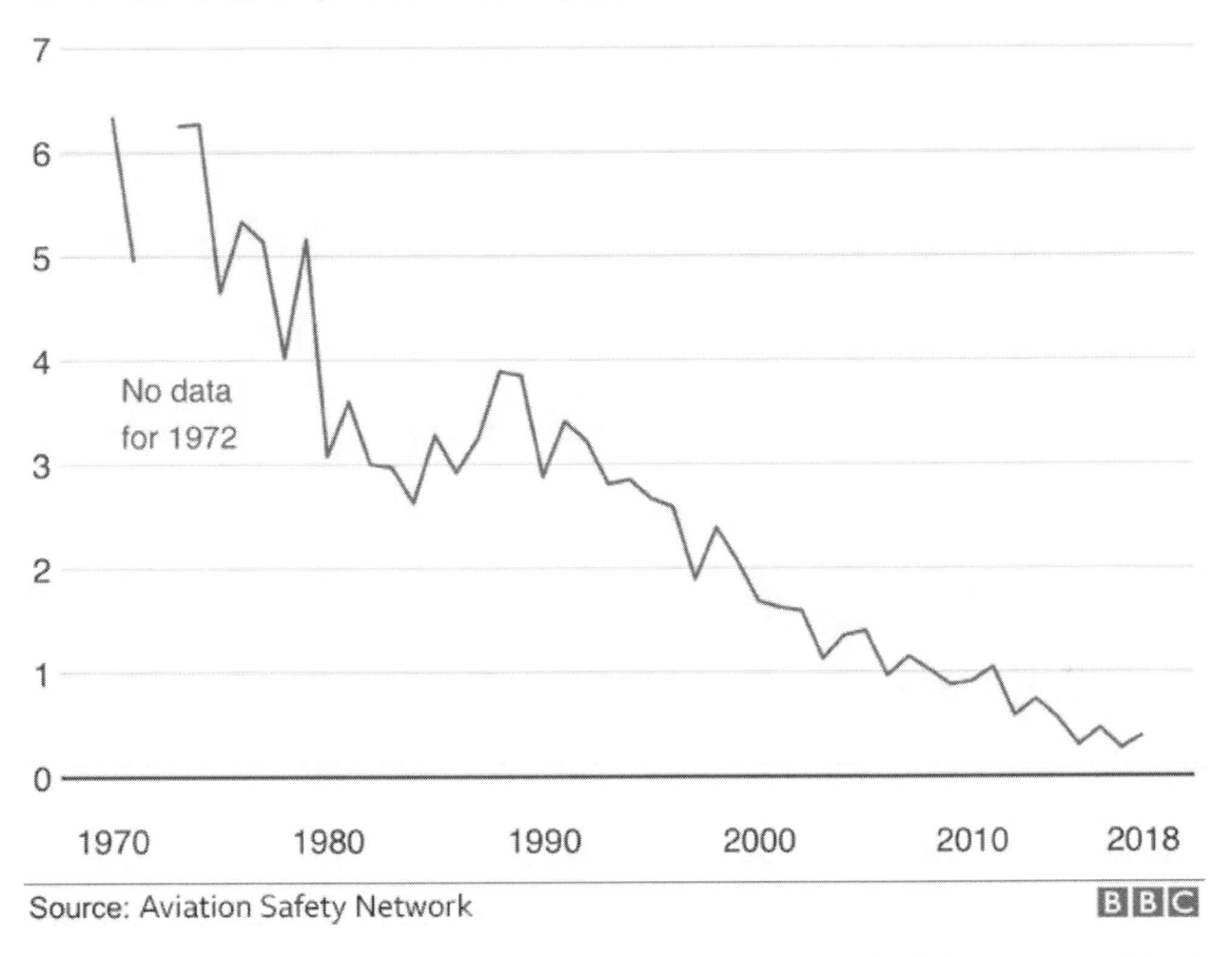

No data for 1972

Source: Aviation Safety Network   BBC

Oh this actually isn't a stock, it is a chart of fatal accidents which have occurred in the aviation industry since the 1970s. Who knew they had head and shoulders too? Let's go over one more chart.

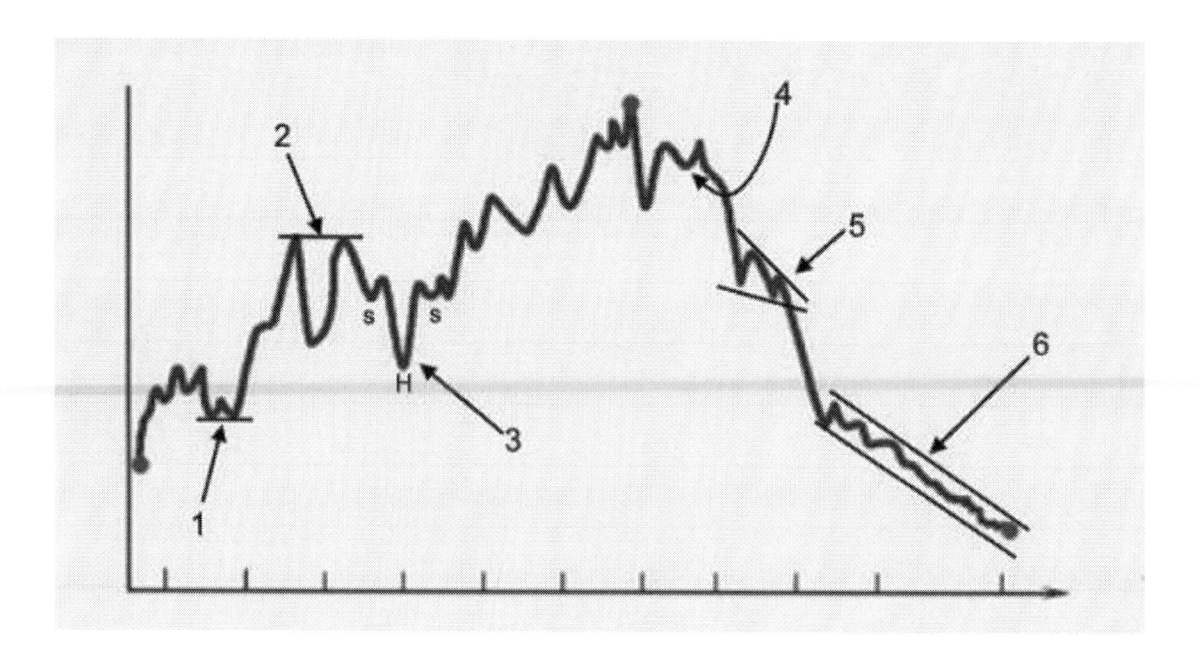

This chart has a ton of patterns all over it, which is why I had to number them. Here are those patterns:

1. Double Bottom
2. Double Top
3. Reverse Head & Shoulders
4. Cup & Handle (failed)
5. Descending Triangle
6. Descending Trendlines

Quite a few patterns we have here, and 5/6 of them were successful! Not too bad. Now let's see what stock we're looking at.

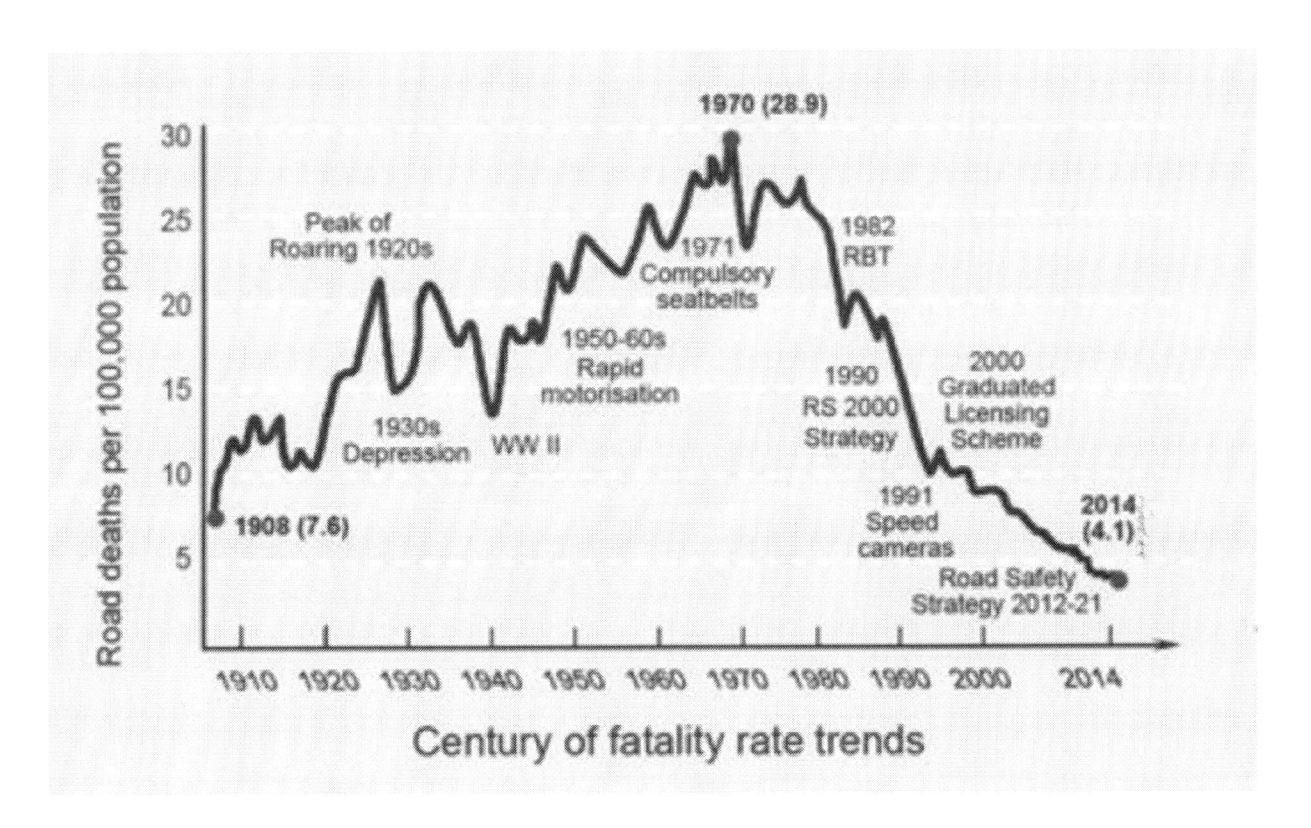

[Chart: Century of fatality rate trends — Road deaths per 100,000 population, from 1908 (7.6) to 2014 (4.1), peaking in 1970 (28.9). Annotations include: Peak of Roaring 1920s; 1930s Depression; WWII; 1950-60s Rapid motorisation; 1971 Compulsory seatbelts; 1982 RBT; 1990 RS 2000 Strategy; 1991 Speed cameras; 2000 Graduated Licensing Scheme; Road Safety Strategy 2012-21.]

Wait, that's not a stock! That's a century's worth of fatality rates in the United States since 1908. The point I'm trying to make here is these supposed unique, rare technical analysis patterns appear in basically any chart you reference. Charts without buyers and sellers, without human psychology, charts which are random. This explains why these patterns are seen in all markets and all time frames. Notice too, all the charts I just referenced are line charts. Once you add in candlesticks with wicks and bodies, technicians now have a number of more places to draw lines, which ends up allowing them to find more patterns.

There is one more chart I want to show you, which I believe is very interesting. Again, I will show you the chart with TA patterns, and then go over the data that created it.

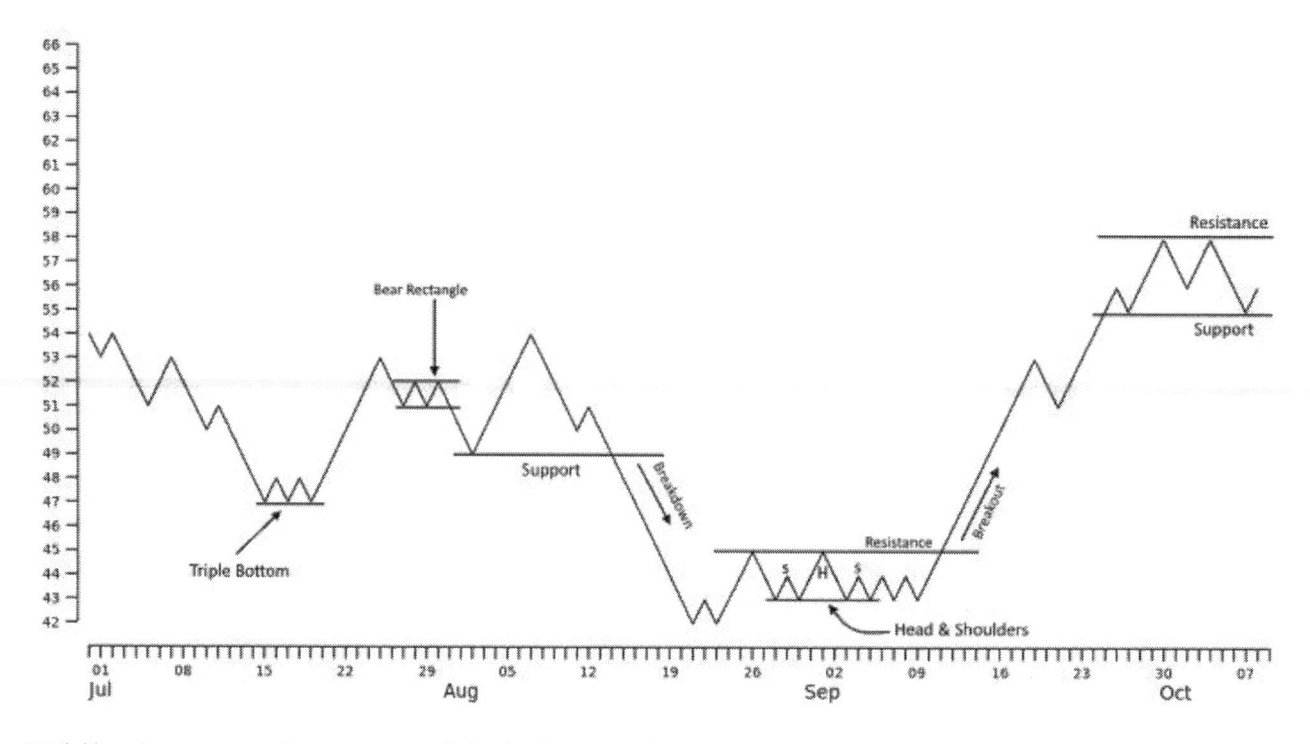

While there may be more, I labeled a number of classic TA patterns which appear on this chart. A triple bottom, bearish rectangle, support, resistance, and a number of other patterns are displayed. So what stock are we looking at?

54

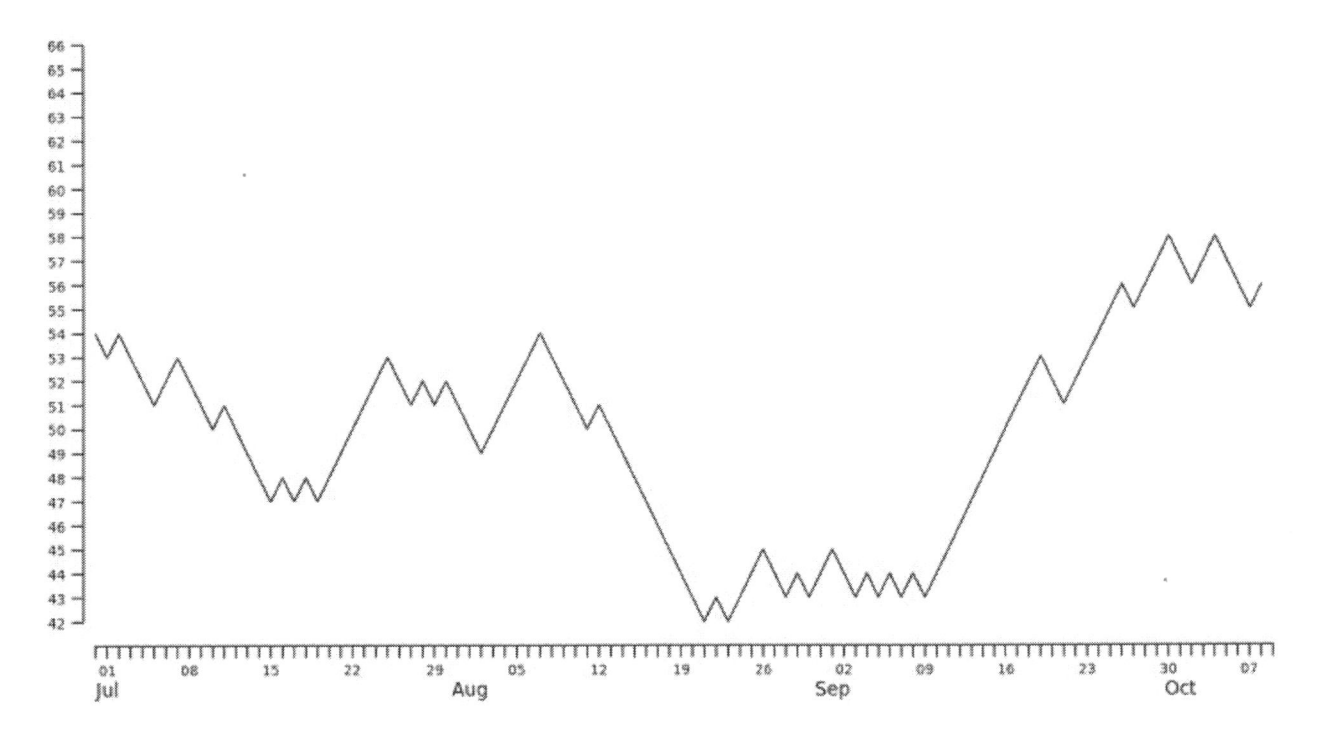

The chart shown is actually the result of flipping a coin every day. It was created by the students of economic professor Burton Malkiel, the economist who created the Random Walk Hypothesis which was mentioned in chapter 1. The students were given a hypothetical stock that was worth $50, and then were told to flip a coin every day. Heads resulted in the stock moving ½ point higher, and tails resulted in the stock moving ½ point lower. As you can see, something as random as flipping a coin resulted in the same pattern formations that CMTs claim are unique to the financial markets. The results from this experiment by Professor Malkiel are quite compelling, in that all these pattern formation could in fact be, like flipping a coin, the result of random chance.

An interesting fact is at the end of the experiment, Malkiel's students took this "stock" chart to a CMT. He told the students they needed to buy the stock immediately because of how compelling of a chart it displayed!

Who Has Acquired Wealth Through TA?

While I've found a couple snippets around the web of supposed professionals who have made their riches from technical analysis, it is not a frequent claim. You find many more cases of traders who have made their money in stocks with time, investing in a diversified portfolio and collecting dividends. My own grandfather started investing with barely any money to his name in quality, dividend stocks. When he retired, he was a millionaire and able to provide for his children and grandkids. Then there's the story of the janitor who left $8,000,000 to his children (linkpony.com/janitor). He had started investing in dividend stocks early in life, and when he died, he was getting $20,000 a month in dividend checks. This isn't magic or rocket science. If you invest in quality companies who pay dividends and leave your money there, you'll eventually become rich.

Stories like these are much more common than stories of someone becoming a millionaire by identifying head and shoulders patterns on an hourly chart of PetSmart. Many more times, you actually hear of people *losing* money with TA. Everyone wants to be rich right now, not in 20 years. However, using a safe, diversified, long-term investing strategy ends up paying off much better and *actually* works.

Considering all the hype around TA, there are many charlatans on the internet who are profiting from the industry. Do a quick search on Amazon or Google, and look at all the technical analysis video courses and books being sold that will make you millions! I could have easily written a similar type of book claiming how technical analysis is

God's gift to earth, and how you will soon live on a private island with Jeffrey Epstein with all your riches. However, I have a little more integrity than that.

It's very easy to make a course showing people how to draw lines on a chart, and then data snooping to draw these lines on charts from the past. And as we just saw, you could have also put these lines on charts of suicides in Illinois and airplane fatalities from the 1970s with the same results.

What none of these courses actually have, and something you'll likely never find, is someone trading with these magical patterns live, in real time, making money consistently each day with TA. This all goes to show that the only people *actually* making money with TA are the ones selling the courses on how to do it, similar to the companies selling the mining equipment during the gold rush. Even the people who created the famous technical analysis indicators like RSI, MACD, etc. didn't acquire wealth from using **their own** indicators, which I'll go over more in the next chapter.

Self-Fulfilling Prophecy

The one caveat that should be mentioned with technical analysis is it can become a self-fulfilling prophecy on heavily traded stocks in common time frames. Look at an ETF like SPY, which has millions of shares traded a day. This is one of the most heavily traded ETFs around, as it correlates with the S&P 500. Considering how many traders are aware of TA, and think it actually works, they are actively looking for patterns that will match their bias. So you may not get it on a 17 minute chart of SPY, however a heavily watched chart of SPY, like the daily chart, may have a tendency to show TA patterns that have a slightly higher tendency to "work."

This is not because these patterns *actually* work, but instead because so many traders are actively looking for them and think they work, and thus affect the course of the ETF itself. However, even with so called self-fulfilling prophecies, it still is a poor system to trade with.

◆ ◆ ◆

Customer Reviews

★★★★★ 38

4.8 out of 5 stars

5 star	██████████	87%
4 star	█	10%
3 star	█	3%
2 star		0%
1 star		0%

See all 38 customer reviews ▸

Share your thoughts with other customers

[Write a customer review]

If you are enjoying this book, could you please leave a review on Amazon? It would be greatly appreciated and allow me to come out with more informative books in the future. A shortened link to the review page is below:

linkpony.com/ta

Chapter 4
The Final Verdicts

Now that we understand both what technicians claim TA can do, as well as the many criticisms of the theory, we will now go over my own philosophy on the subject. I will go over the parts of technical analysis that I feel are complete bullshit, the parts that are plausible, and the parts that seem to be effective.

◆ ◆ ◆

TA That Is Bullshit

First, I'd like to go over the patterns that are complete rubbish. You may already have a sense of what items will be on this list from what I've mentioned in previous chapters.

All Chart Patterns

The cup and handle, head and shoulders, double top, falling wedge, and all other patterns. Basically all patterns that are drawn on a chart are complete nonsense. As shown, these patterns appear in all charts and are not limited to the stock market. They appear in suicide rates, crime statistics, airplane accidents, etc. Meaning there is no reason to believe they are somehow unique to the stock market, buyers and sellers, or human psychology. Not only this, as shown with the coin flip experiment, these patterns are most likely the result of random occurrences.

I want you think for a second though. Let's say hypothetically these patterns were real. Say we have a head and shoulders pattern beginning to appear on a chart. What on earth would make that pattern continue in its "proper" direction? Is the energy of the universe making that head and shoulders complete itself? Are God's hands coming down on the chart, pulling on the stock price? Thinking logically about it, there is no reason why the stock will follow the pattern specified, or any pattern for that matter, as the stock market is simply buyers and sellers randomly trading stocks.

Fibonacci Retracement/Projection

I reserved a spot in the book for this preposterous tool. Originally, Fibonacci retracement tools just used the 38.2% and 61.8% lines. However, most charting software nowadays have also placed a 50% and 23.6% line into the Fibonacci retracement tool. As such, you now have four lines between a randomly assigned high and low point on a chart.

The first issue we run into with this tool is where should you place your high and low point? There are literally hundreds of high and low points on a chart that you could choose, so which one is correct? In the daily chart of Tesla (TSLA) on the next page, I have drawn 5 Fibonacci retracement lines, with plausible high and low points.

Look how much of a mess this chart is! Which one is correct? And while I only used 5 Fibonacci lines, I could have easily plotted more. Typical of TA, there is no "correct location" to set your high and low point, and it becomes a guessing game. Let me show you what it would have looked like had I drawn just one Fibonacci retracement line though.

61

Here I drew a pretty reasonable Fibonacci retracement line. The Fibonacci retracement tool then plots 4 dotted lines (23.6%, 38.2%, 50%, 61.8%) between the high and low locations. Think about this. Four completely random dotted lines are plotted between a high and low point of a stock. Based on sheer probability, of course the stock is going to pivot around at least one of them! This is completely random though, and has nothing to do with the laws of nature or the "golden ratio." It's very likely the additional 50% and 23.6% line were added for this exact reason, in that it gives more probability of the tool working, and for marketing purposes.

And it's the same exact thing with "Fibonacci projection," and the many other Fibonacci tools that have spun off from Fibonacci retracement. They share the same issue of randomly picking a bottom/top, and then data snooping to determine favorable results.

Elliott Wave Theory

It's hard for me to even write this section out because of how absurd of a theory this is. That this theory is even considered by chartists baffles my mind. As I'm sure you've reasoned by now, there are a number of flaws with this theory, and I cannot find any redeeming qualities surrounding it.

To begin, Elliott himself was kind of "out there." Not only did he believe in the Fibonacci retracement theory, he also believed his wave theory applied to all human behaviors, not just the stock market. He wrote a book titled *Nature's Law – The Secret of the Universe*, which details how EWT applies to all aspects of human life. I'm not saying this guy was egotistical, but I am saying he was most likely pretty wacky. As in he probably also believed in water dowsing, crystal balls, and magic spells. While he did predict a market bottom, it's very possible he got lucky; the stock market can only go up or down.

There is no information regarding Mr. Elliott making profits from his wave theory, except for the books and articles he wrote about it. There is a company which continues to propagate his theory called "Elliott Wave International." For just $200 a month, you can subscribe to their newsletter. While enticing, the company has no track record displayed, or any indication their subscription service beats the market, or is even profitable.

The big issue with this theory is how subjective it is. Similar to Fibonacci retracement, you have to try and pick where the 5-3 waves are on a chart at random. This may be possible with data snooping, but try doing this in the real time. Not only that, the theory is also supposed to work in any time frame and in any market. As in it should work on a 5 minute, 6 minute, and 7 minute chart of oil, gold, and APPL. Let me show you an example of "Elliott Wave" charts I've found through my research.

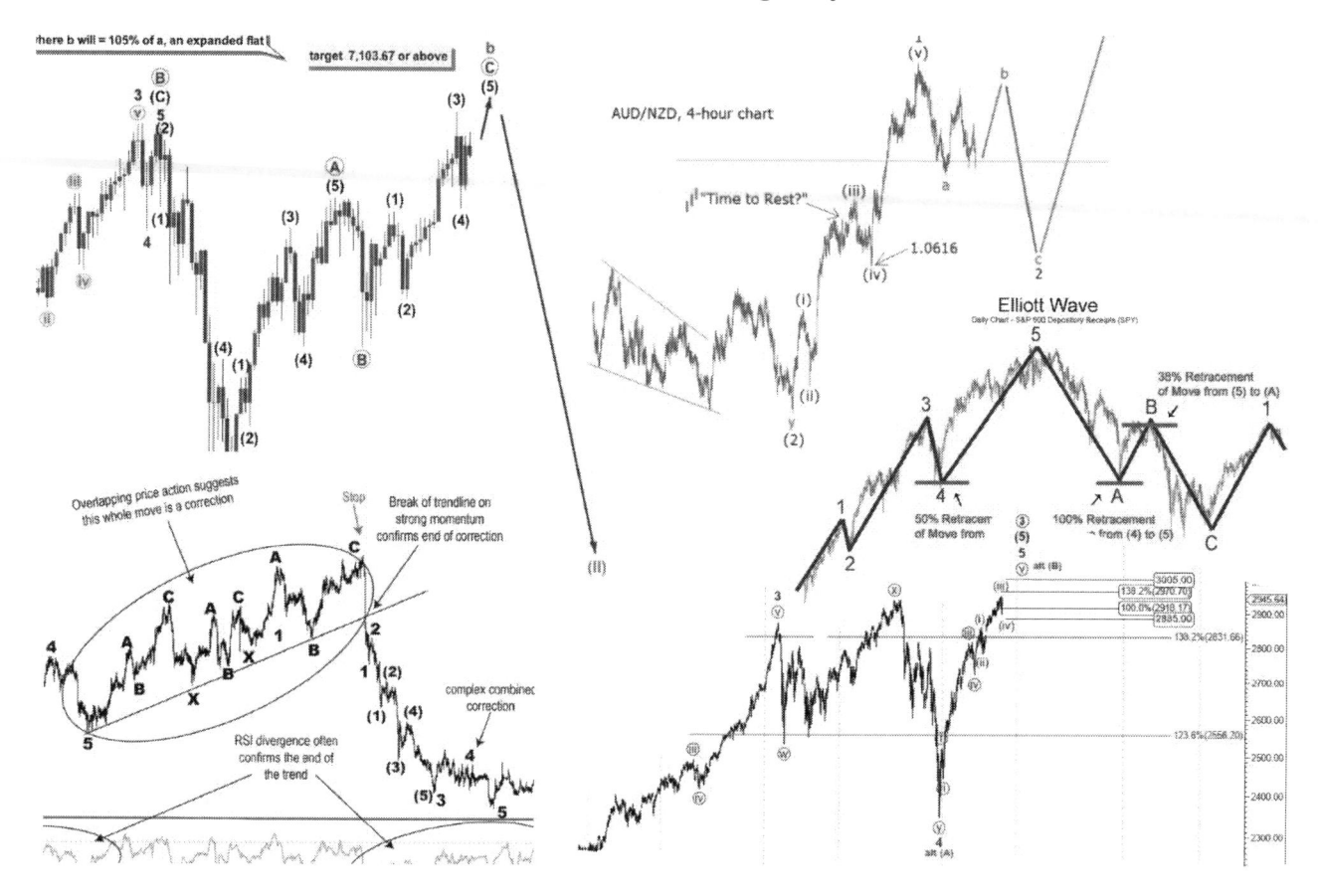

As customary with data snooping and confirmation bias, technicians draw lines anywhere they can to make the EWT fit on their chart. As you can see from the picture, many times they completely ignore certain "waves" because they did not fit in with what they wanted the pattern to look like. Out of all the TA theories in this book, this one is the most ridiculous. There is no reason the universe makes stocks move in 5-3 patterns.

Bollinger Bands

Testing out this indicator myself many times, it's seems rather poor. Sometimes it works, but many times it doesn't. In my experience Bollinger Bands actually work less than a coin flip, with a ton of false signals that could have disastrous results. Unlike other indicators which use moving averages or closing prices, Bollinger Bands are essentially using general math (standard deviations), as a basis for their predictions. Let me show you a common occurrence with Bollinger Bands that could lead to dire results.

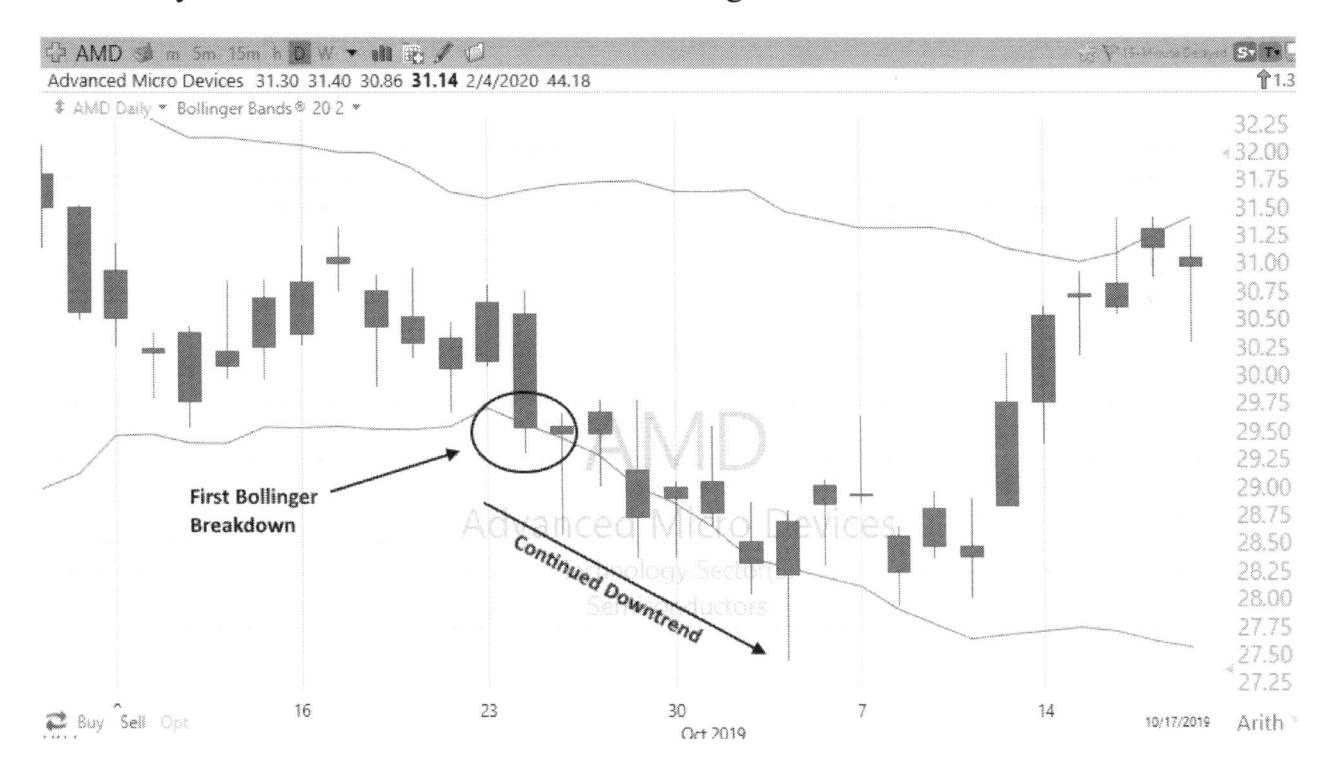

Here the stock breaks the bottom Bollinger Band, which would be considered a buy signal. The stock then continues trending downward for many days before finally reverting back inside the Bollinger Bands. Had you actually bought at the first "buy signal," you would have of course lost quite a bit of money.

Then there is the claim that "contracting" Bollinger Bands result in a breakout. While this may be true, the issue is the breakout direction is not known, meaning the stock could shoot up or down. This results in guessing and hoping for the correct direction. Not a very good stock strategy. For a $200 monthly subscription, I'd be happy to tell you a stock could go up or down!

And in regards to the creator, John Bollinger, he appears to just be riding the wave of his invention. His Bollinger Bands book has been translated into 11 languages, and he also sells additional books and video courses on his website. All of which he makes a profit from.

In terms of actually using his Bollinger Bands tool to make money, it doesn't seem he does that well. I was able to obtain a profit chart from John's hedge fund, Bollinger Capital Management (BCM). He has two portfolio options investors can subscribe to: BCM Balanced and BCM Growth.

Year	S&P 500	BCM Balanced	BCM Growth
2000	-9.73%	4.5%	1.8%
2001	-11.75%	-4.4%	-5.7%
2002	-21.59%	-11.7%	-10.6%
2003	28.18%	20.3%	21.1%
2004	10.70%	8.8%	9.5%
2005	4.83%	6.9%	9.4%
2006	15.85%	10.8%	17.6%
2007	5.14%	2.5%	7.9%
2008	-36.81%	-37.4%	-40.3%
2009	26.36%	27.4%	22.4%
2010	15.06%	22.3%	22.2%
2011	1.89%	-10.5%	-10.3%
2012	15.99%	10.9%	9.3%
2013	32.31%	7.7%	10.5%
2014	13.46%	2.2%	3.6%
2015	1.25%	-5.3%	-4.7%
2016	12.00%	15.9%	14.6%
2017	21.70%	19.5%	22.3%
Total Since 2000	124.84%	74.6%	91.4%

Over 18 years, neither of his portfolios were able beat the general market. His highest returning portfolio, the BCM growth, returned a total of 91.4% over these 17 years. Compare this to the S&P 500 which returned 125% in these 18 years. Not only was John unable to beat the market, he lost quite a bit more than the general market on many occasions. A tool that **works** should consistently work and consistently beat the market. John Bollinger and his Bollinger Bands do not accomplish this.

Divergence

As we went over in chapter 1, divergence is when the trend in an indicator (MACD, RSI, etc.) disagrees with the stock trend, meaning a direction change is supposed to occur in the stock. Of course, many times this "divergence" principal does not work. This actually works less than a coin flip, as sometimes the stock continues its trend, sometimes it stays flat, and sometimes it reverses its trend. As in it's random. Let me show you an example.

Here we have an example with the daily chart of Intel (INTC). In this scenario, the RSI chart is showing an uptrend while the stock chart is showing a downtrend. Based on divergence theory, the stock should reverse trend and start increasing in price. Of course that doesn't happen. While this may be considered cherry picking on my part, scenarios like this are quite common with the "divergence" principle, and the stock either goes up, down, or stays flat. As in you have a better chance of choosing red or black on a roulette table than using the TA divergence principal.

◆ ◆ ◆

TA That is Plausible

RSI, Stochastics, MACD

All three of these indicators are trying to measure overbought/oversold conditions. I definitely do think a stock can fall into this scenario. A stock is only worth a certain amount based on its fundamentals (revenue, P/E ratio, etc). If too many people buy a stock, it can become overvalued, and as such, eventually retraces back to a fair price. And it's the same when a stock sells off too much, as it becomes undervalued and eventually retraces to a fair price. Look at stocks like Beyond Meat (BYND) and Tilray (TLRY). These stocks went wildly higher after their IPOs, becoming heavily overbought. They then crashed back down to earth to much more reasonable valuations within a few months. That is why it seems plausible an indicator could in fact measure oversold/overbought conditions.

An issue we face with these indicators is though, while they sometimes work, they sometimes don't. They can give false signals that could potentially lose traders money.

For example, a stock may experience an RSI over 70 for many days, even weeks, before coming back down. It's one thing to look at a chart and data snoop for favorable results, but it's another thing to be using these signals in real time. It would be hard to imagine a trader could potentially use any of these signals by themselves and make consistent profits. However, it may be possible with some type of very concrete trading system in place to make these work. Possibly only buying stocks that are in a certain trend, using stop-losses, confirmation candles, etc. This would still only be useful though for speculative, swing or day trading type strategies. Long term studies have shown these indicators fail to beat a standard, buy and hold portfolio. Not only that, you would have to constantly monitor your account, pay short term capital gains taxes when you sell, and would experience a lot of whiplash using these indicators long term.

Something to note is these indicators may be beneficial as a *supplement* to traders. For example, let's say you find a favorable stock you want to buy which has been sinking in price. You may decide to wait until the RSI reaches under 30 to buy said stock, which the fundamentals indicate is a good investment. This way you can hopefully get in near the bottom of the range. As in you are looking at the fundamentals first, before then reaching out to an indicator for additional confirmation.

There is one other thing I feel I should mention about these indicators. These indicators all appear to have been invented by very intelligent people. However, after extensive research, I could not find anything in regards to any of the inventors (J. Welles Wilder, George Lane, Gerald Appel) making riches with their indicators. Similar to John Bollinger, I find that they seem to have written books about them, performed seminars and training, but did not actually acquire wealth through *their own* indicators. To me, that does seem odd.

Volume

Volume seems to be another indicator that could plausibly help predict the direction of a stock. It appears to be an indication of a trend continuing. As in, an uptrend with buying volume tends to continue so as long as volume continues increasing, and the same with a downtrend with selling volume. All it means is many buyers or sellers are coming into the equation. Of course when more people buy a stock, it increases in price. And when more people sell a stock, it decreases. So it is plausible to use volume as an indication of when a trend will continue. Like the other indicators though, it doesn't work all the time.

◆ ◆ ◆

TA That Appears to Work

Trends

While not referencing trendlines specifically, trends themselves tend to be a fairly reliable indicator in the stock market. There is a common saying in the stock world that "the trend is your friend." As in, the long term trend is a reliable way to gauge the general direction of the stock. This makes sense.

Let's look at a company like Apple. They've been in an uptrend for many years, but there is a fundamental reason for this. They produce quality products, products which consumers continuously buy, and this in turn produces profitable earnings and lots of revenue for the company. The trend, which you can see on a chart, is just the direct result of Apple being a good company. Apple is not controlled by the chart or going up because the technical patterns are making it. It is instead trending upward as a result of

Apple's fundamentals.

Moving Averages

The thing about moving averages is they are not patterns or shapes that appear on a chart. They are instead the last "X" number of periods of the stock's price, expressed as a smooth line on a chart. Common moving averages include the 50 day, 100 day, and 200 day moving averages. It is what is known as a "lagging" indicator, meaning it trails the real time price action of the stock.

Sometimes stocks will "bounce" off these moving averages. They are of course not magical. I think it is a combination of multiple people watching them (self-fulfilling prophecy), as well as a stock being in "oversold" or "overbought" conditions. Many traders also determine if they should buy or sell a stock based on where its moving average is located. For example, if a stock is above its 50 MA, it can be viewed as in a bullish trend and still a good buy. However, if the stock moves below its 50 MA, it may now be considered to be trending downward, and the trader may sell it. MAs directly correlate with trends.

Certain moving average crossovers are also fairly dependable, with the death cross and golden cross being two examples. Again, these are lagging indicators which are just showing you the movement and trend of a stock. They are not magical patterns you have to try and find on a chart; they are numerical and quantitative. That is what makes them much more reliable and believable than other forms of TA.

Bonus Chapter
Japanese Candlesticks

Japanese candlesticks, the candlesticks commonly shown in "candlestick" charts, have their own mystical philosophy I'd like to go over here in this bonus chapter. I want to first clarify that I am not purposing candlesticks themselves aren't beneficial. I frequently use candlestick charts when looking at stocks. They provide more information than regular line charts, as they display the high, low, open, and close of the day, as well as if the stock went up or down on the day. What I am purposing is the patterns they form, which I will soon show you, are most likely also random and have no correlation to future price movement.

Similar to TA theory, there is a theory that certain patterns that appear in candlesticks can predict future price movements. Let me show you a chart of the most common candlestick patterns.

CANDLESTICK CHEAT SHEET

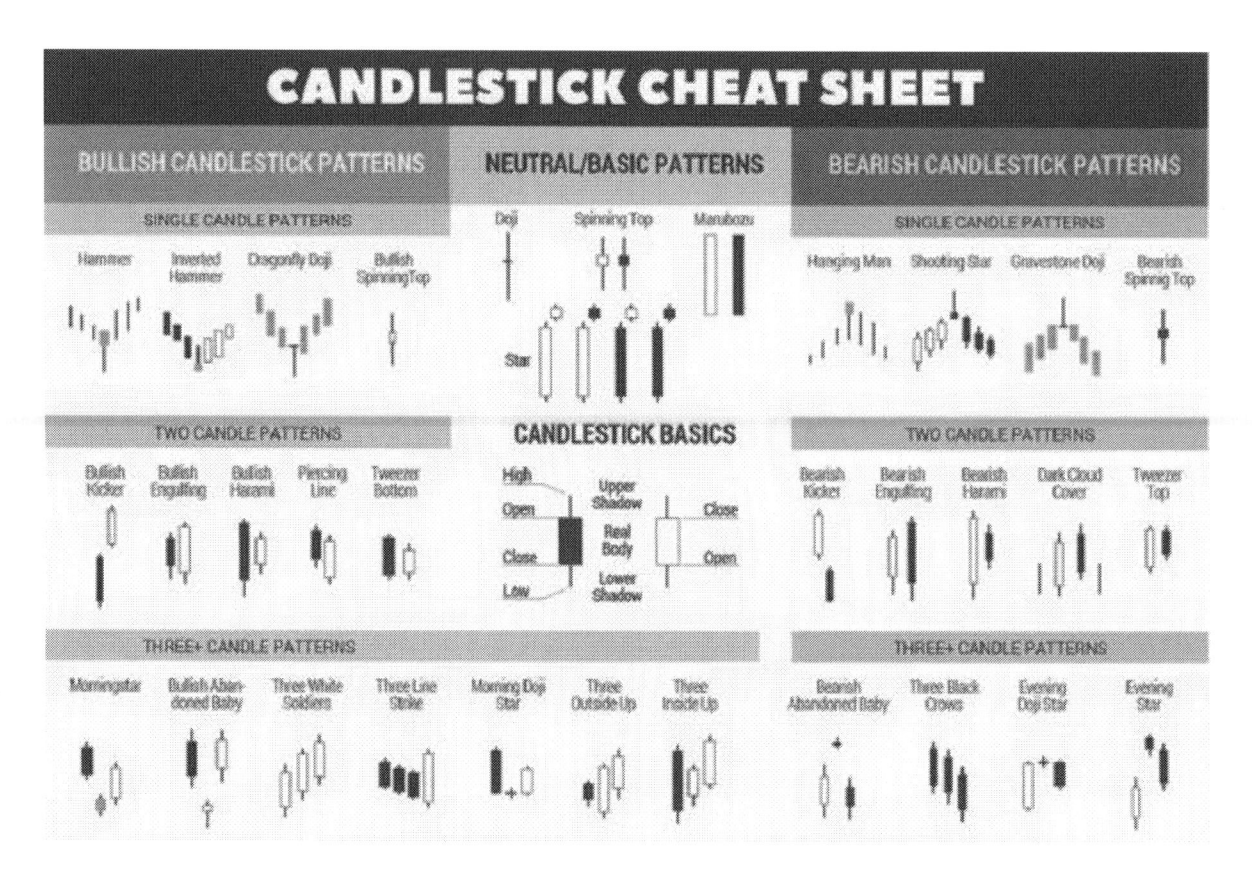

Like technical analysis, there are bullish, neutral, and bearish candlestick patterns. They are also said to work in all markets and timeframes, which include stocks, commodities, forex, etc. The issues that we run into with trying to gauge future stock prices from candlestick formations are similar to the issues we ran into with technical analysis. That is, there is nothing quantitative causing these patterns to work, and using them correctly becomes an "art" and not a science. The CMT association also includes candlesticks in their $1,500 course (go figure).

Let's look at a gravestone doji, which is located in the top right section of the picture above. This is a pattern commonly touted by candlestickers to predict a bearish reversal in the stock price. I would compare it to a double top pattern in TA. And like TA, it's a pattern on a chart and there is nothing "making" it happen. Why should one day of more sellers predict the next day of stock movement? What if the next day, more buyers come in? Why can't they? There is nothing here in regards to fundamentals. There is no oversold or overbought conditions. It's just a candle formation displayed on a chart.

And of course, just like TA, you can use data snooping, confirmation bias, etc. to "prove" that candlesticks work. But of course there are many fake outs and false patterns that occur with Japanese candlesticks as well. Unfortunately, most data un-related to stocks (airplane crashes, suicide rates, etc.) is displayed in the form of a line chart. However, if this data could somehow be displayed in candlestick formation, I would argue the same candlestick patterns would appear on those charts as well. You of course are welcome to try candlesticks yourself, as I have done in the past, however you will find just like most of TA, they are also complete rubbish.

There are a couple facts which add support to my claim that predicting stock movements with candlestick patterns is a fraudulent practice. The first fact would be there are no traders, as least not through my own extensive research, with proven wealth acquired through candlestick trading. What I *instead* find is, similar to technical analysis, many books and video courses that claim to teach the art of "Japanese Candlesticks." As in, people making money selling the theory.

One individual, who has multiple candlestick chart books on Amazon, some with over 300 reviews, refuses to release his tax information or trading results when asked. Yet he still cashes in on seminars, books, and subscriptions on the subject, claiming to be an expert. And after a little research, I found out this person is also a CMT… how about that! A non-biased review of this person can be found on TradingSchools.org. If you search for "candlestick charts" on Amazon, and then look through the authors, you should be able to determine who I'm talking about pretty quickly.

The second fact is, unlike 30 years ago when Japanese candlesticks originally appeared, computers can now back test the theorized candlestick patterns to see if they actually work better than general probability and chance. And as it turns out, these "candlestick patterns" don't work. They work no better than chance at predicting the direction of a stock. A more detailed explanation of this study can be found here, in the "Back Testing Candlestick Patterns" section of the page (linkpony.com/pattern).

So it can be stated fairly conclusively that, similar to just about all other aspects of TA, candlestick patterns are also bullshit.

Conclusion

I hope this book has opened your eyes to what technical analysis truly is, and the reasons most of it is complete nonsense. While technical analysis may have originally been created with good intentions, it doesn't seem to have ever been a successful method of trading. And like other get rich quick schemes, technical analysis has gone the way of crooks selling dreams. You can subscribe to their trades, chatrooms, etc. and be a successful technical analysis trader just like them!

While I don't feel the stock market is *completely* random, much of it is. You probably would have better luck flipping a coin than using technical analysis patterns on a chart, as it can easily be compared to tarot cards, crystal balls, or astrology, as famed economist Malkiel has noted. Traders who've claimed to have used technical analysis to gain wealth most likely used much more than pure TA as their guide, and luck, timing, insider knowledge, and a host of other factors could have added to their success.

Of course, looking at a stock on a chart still has its benefits. The chart shows you the momentum of the stock, and as indicated, there are a few redeeming qualities of technical analysis, such as moving averages and trends. So while there are some benefits to technical analysis, and some traders and hedge funds do use it, it's probably best to be used as a supplement to your trading, and not the primary component.

What I have found, and try to preach, is the best way to make consistent income in the stock market is with a long term, buy and hold strategy that uses the general market as a backbone. This has helped many more people generate wealth with stocks than with technical analysis, and it will work for you too!

◆ ◆ ◆

If you enjoyed this book, you may also like...

Dividend Investing for Everyone

A Beginners Guide to Building Your Wealth Through Dividend Stocks

Shortened Link to Book

linkpony.com/div

Make companies **pay you** to own their stocks! In *Dividend Investing for Everyone*, Tim Morris goes over everything you need to know about dividends, and why they are one of Wall Street's best kept secrets when it comes to long term investing. Dividends provide substantially more income than stocks alone, and when you're done reading this book, you'll know exactly why!

The 20% Solution

A Long Term Investment Strategy that Averages 20.13% Per Year

Shortened Link to Book
linkpony.com/20

You read that right, **20.13% per year!** This strategy, which Tim has coined *The 20% Solution*, requires just 4 trades a year. And of those 4 trades, very little is destined to capital gains tax. This book includes 30 years of history of this strategy in action, with charts and figures to back it up. Go to the link above to find out more!

Printed in Great Britain
by Amazon